T0352881

OPEN YOUR
Third Eye

About the Author

Jiulio Consiglio (Ontario, Canada) is a spiritual teacher and author who focuses on the transformative power of inner stillness, the mind-body-spirit connection, and the development of psychic abilities. His message is that there is life beyond fear and incessant thinking, and it is found in the dimension of inner stillness. Jiulio currently offers his consciousness-based teachings to individuals and groups.

To Write to the Author

If you wish to contact the author or would like more information about this book, please write to the author in care of Llewellyn Worldwide Ltd. and we will forward your request. Both the author and publisher appreciate hearing from you and learning of your enjoyment of this book and how it has helped you. Llewellyn Worldwide Ltd. cannot guarantee that every letter written to the author can be answered, but all will be forwarded. Please write to:

Jiulio Consiglio
� Llewellyn Worldwide
2143 Wooddale Drive
Woodbury, MN 55125-2989

Please enclose a self-addressed stamped envelope for reply, or $1.00 to cover costs. If outside the U.S.A., enclose an international postal reply coupon.

Many of Llewellyn's authors have websites with additional information and resources. For more information, please visit our website at http://www.llewellyn.com.

OPEN YOUR
Third Eye

Activate Your Sixth Chakra & Develop Your Psychic Abilities

JIULIO CONSIGLIO

Llewellyn Publications
Woodbury, Minnesota

FIRST EDITION
First Printing, 2021

Book design by Samantha Peterson
Chakra figure by Mary Ann Zapalac
Cover design by Kevin R. Brown

Library of Congress Cataloging-in-Publication Data
Names: Consiglio, Jiulio, author.
Title: Open your third eye : activate your sixth chakra & develop your psychic abilities / by Jiulio Consiglio.
Description: First edition. | Woodbury, MN : Llewellyn Worldwide, Ltd, 2021. | Summary: "Filled with simple yet effective exercises and meditations, this practical guide provides everything you need to open your third eye and improve your innate psychic abilities"— Provided by publisher.
Identifiers: LCCN 2021007028 (print) | LCCN 2021007029 (ebook) | ISBN 9780738767093 (paperback) | ISBN 9780738768069 (ebook)
Subjects: LCSH: Psychic ability. | Chakras.
Classification: LCC BF1031 .C5898 2021 (print) | LCC BF1031 (ebook) | DDC 133.8—dc23
LC record available at https://lccn.loc.gov/2021007028
LC ebook record available at https://lccn.loc.gov/2021007029

Llewellyn Publications
A Division of Llewellyn Worldwide Ltd.
2143 Wooddale Drive
Woodbury, MN 55125-2989
www.llewellyn.com

Printed in the United States of America

Other Books by Jiulio Consiglio

Challenge Your Thoughts
The Healing Frequency

This book is dedicated to my brother Steve, a powerful force who left this earth much too early. You taught me what inner strength is, which has enabled me to face whatever presented in my life. I still feel your strength and guidance to this day, big brother.

CONTENTS

EXERCISE AND MEDITATION LIST

ACKNOWLEDGMENTS

I want to thank and acknowledge Source, The All That Is, for reminding me who I really am. You have never failed me.

To Mom and Dad. Thank you for everything. I love you both so very much.

To my grandmother Gerlanda: You demonstrated and taught me the power of faith. I still feel your love each and every day.

A tremendous amount of gratitude to my editors, Amy Glaser and Nicole Borneman. Amy, you were my initial contact with Llewellyn. Thank you for your support, expertise, guidance, and kindness. I am beyond grateful. Nicole, thank you for your guidance, professionalism, understanding, and insight in preparing the manuscript. Your work on this project has been greatly appreciated. Thank you both for helping me evolve as a writer.

And finally, to all the staff at Llewellyn Worldwide that work behind the scenes making it possible for writers to publish their work, thank you. A thousand blessings to all of you.

INTRODUCTION

There isn't a human being on the planet that doesn't have some level of psychic ability—it's simply encoded within us. It is just a part of who we are as spiritual beings. I should mention this right from the start: it's not so much that the third eye and all its spiritual faculties are dormant within us, but rather that most people are unaware of it and its capabilities due to the veil of this world and the physical senses. We have been given a very powerful gift, but without opening it—without activating it and developing it—we close ourselves off to potential, possibility, and fulfillment of our life's purpose. In this book, I will address what the sixth chakra is, how to prepare for its activation, and which exercises and methods will bring you closer to utilizing its full potential. It is my hope that as we journey together into the dimension of spirit and the reality of pure consciousness, you realize the following: what you desire is already within you.

The sixth chakra, or third eye, is one of the seven main energy wheels found within the subtle body. Located between the eyebrows, it serves as the seat of clarity, intuition, wisdom, and inner knowing. The third eye is the gateway to insight. When this channel is clear, its potential becomes active. The result is a heightened sixth sense that can empower your life in many ways, from being able to access your inner intuitive compass to navigating through life more clearly to reading the energy around others to help them heal.

Third Eye Alignment

In my experience, being in tune with an activated third eye has been a conscious awareness of being in alignment in mind, body, and soul. The highest self is directly experienced through inner stillness, and its reflection is a deep sense of well-being. This well-being results in freely flowing energy—an inner fluidity, if you will—which then reflects in the world around you.

The focus of this book will be on the activation, development, and mastery of this chakra. This spiritual faculty will enable you to further expand your awareness and consciousness so that you may enhance your psychic abilities. As we move forward together, I will impart wisdom and understanding because it all leads to clarity, which is the seat of the third eye. With every insight offered, you cannot help but raise your vibration, bringing you a step closer to the fulfillment of desire—which, in this case, is the further development of your psychic abilities through an activated third eye. The understanding offered will also spill over to psychic and paranormal phenomena based on some of my own personal experiences. Now, let us remain focused on the task at hand, which is your personal spiritual growth as you come closer to realizing your highest potential through the sixth chakra.

The spiritual faculty you require to access higher dimensions of consciousness and to read and interpret energy with clarity is already yours. It's just partially or mostly covered by layers of emotion and human conditioning, depending on your level of self-understanding. The more spiritually aware you are, the more aligned you are with your sixth sense. In other words, the closer you are to center, your authentic spiritual self, the more in alignment you will be with your psychic abilities. Everything is energy, and the more you realize this, the easier it will be to understand that being human does not for one moment diminish the fact that you are a spiritual being capable of accessing information beyond the normal five senses.

Pre- and Post-Activation

I am now going to discuss what an activated third eye looks and feels like versus an inactivated one. Allow me to paint a picture of the two. Operating through this activated chakra results in profound clarity and wisdom, which is a result of enhanced intuition based in hyperawareness. In other words, there's no more second guessing of one's intuition, and there's no more dismissing of psychic events: "Oh, it was just a hunch" type of thing. It's also a direct knowing and feeling of oneness; an experience of being one with everything and everyone.

An inactivated third eye doesn't close the door on psychic experiences or feelings of oneness. There are still episodes of intuition and moments of feeling unified with everything and everyone, but these are limited in their potential to fully express all of its capabilities. There are moments of clarity and wisdom, aha moments if you will, just not to the degree of an activated chakra. Basically, in this experience, one is more grounded in this reality, third-dimensional reality.

Many different roads can lead to sixth chakra activation. For example, it can take place through intention, which includes the implementation of spiritual techniques such as meditation and mindfulness; practicing being in a mindset of allowing for its blossoming to take place; cultivating spiritual faculties by focusing on the energy body; or by a spontaneous awakening following several personal adversities. Regardless of how it happens, gradually or through urgency, desire seems to be a common ingredient. Again, the focus of this book will be on what you can do to create an atmosphere to allow for sixth chakra activation, because ultimately the timing of your awakening to sixth chakra reality is all in the hands of synchronicity. When you are ready for it, it will happen.

My Sixth Chakra Activation

Before we get started, I'm going to share the events that led to my third eye activation. By the time I had reached the age of thirty-two, it appeared that I was living quite a successful life. It was 2002 and I was working in my chosen profession as a dental hygienist and educator. I had just gotten married, had a nice car, and lived in a nice house. On the surface, it seemed like I had everything. Yet despite it all, I couldn't help but sense that something was missing.

The last decade or so had been difficult for me. I have always been incredibly sensitive to emotional energy—mine and that of others. Since the age of nineteen, I struggled with nagging feelings of anxiety and couldn't understand why. I'm not a huge fan of labels of any kind, but it would seem that I fit the description of an empath. On top of that, at the age of twenty-four, I lost my one and only older brother to cancer, and that experience left me with many unanswered questions, questions that continued to haunt me.

A few years later I got married and, just when it seemed like I had it all, things started to fall apart. In the fall of 2003, my marriage abruptly came to an end after just fifteen months because we realized we were both unhappy. About a year later, in the winter of 2004, I was diagnosed with cancer. I was told that surgery and radiation were required. By this point, the universe really had my attention. You would think that a life-threatening diagnosis was perhaps enough to cause a spontaneous sixth chakra activation within me, but it didn't—it only left me more frustrated.

The final straw came to me in the form of a night terror in the fall of 2005 while I was in remission. At around 3:00 a.m., I awoke to the feeling of a dark, negative presence hovering over me. As I glanced down at my sheets, I immediately noticed them being pulled off me. Shocked more than anything, I jumped out of bed, went downstairs, said a few prayers, and fell asleep on the couch. The next morning I headed back to my bedroom, and as I reached the threshold, I still sensed that dark entity. I walked past it and told it, in no uncertain terms, to get lost. I jumped in the shower and, feeling as low as I had ever felt, I called out to Source Energy for guidance and assistance.

A few weeks went by. One day, while nearing the end of my shift, one of my patients cancelled their appointment. I did what I normally would do: I got in my car, drove a short distance, and tried to relax. This time, however, I had a book with me that I had been reading called *Change Your Brain, Change Your Life* by Dr. Daniel Amen. I began to recall one of the lines from the book when all of a sudden a clear, distinct, and audible voice spoke to me and said, "Challenge your thoughts!"

In that instant, the center of my forehead was activated by a powerful feeling of vibration. I automatically began to shut down every negative or limiting thought that attempted to come into my consciousness. As I turned my head to look around me, I can recall the profound clarity I experienced in that moment, when everything made sense all at once.

I knew something life changing was taking place, that I had engaged some kind of force within me, but the thought of having activated the third eye hadn't crossed my mind. At that time, I knew very little of chakras and their potential. Even though I didn't know exactly what was happening, I was astonished and excited all at once. I felt my prayers were being answered, finally.

I am still boggled as to how I managed to do this, but I returned to work to finish my last patient. As I was working away, my now-activated third eye was still vibrating and shutting down anything unlike itself, anything unlike unconditional love. It was operating on autopilot, with no effort on my part.

I finished work and began to drive home in a bad rainstorm. I was still experiencing the now-activated force in my forehead as negativity tried to reach my awareness. I got home, lay down on the couch, and, feeling quite emotionally spent, felt a great feeling of letting go. In that moment, I closed my eyes and uttered the words, "Just let me die." These words seemed to come from what I would describe as a space of complete surrender—surrender to life, death, and Source Energy. I then popped out of my body for what felt like only a few moments before coming back to awareness. To this day, I am still unsure how long I was out of my body. When I came to, I realized that my life had now changed course toward the light of consciousness in a very extraordinary way.

As a result of my sixth chakra activation, every aspect of my life changed for the better. For the first time in my life, I began to really experience a deep sense of well-being, understanding, and inner peace. After undergoing the "dying before you die" event, I came to experience understanding and knowing. I *was* those things. I intuitively knew after this experience that I had activated my third eye and that its activation was the key to the quantum field. I had shed my conditioned, egoic self and by doing that, I realized my oneness with Source Energy on a conscious level; this is how I shifted from a lack of awareness to heightened awareness and understanding. Clarity became my friend and I realized the power that comes from living in the moment.

In the weeks that followed my activation, I experienced mystical events, including one that entailed a vision of self-healing that impacted me on so many levels. In the vision, I approached a version of myself that was sitting in a wheelchair. I then placed my hand on the other me sitting in the wheelchair, healing myself. It was an emotional and energetic healing all in one, and it spoke volumes to me about the potential of the quantum field.

It wasn't long after that I began experiencing automatic writing. The only way I can explain it is that what I was writing was not coming from human consciousness. I was beginning to write about the spiritual realm, the subtle body, chakras, and so much more.

I held my first speaking engagement on the power of consciousness within the first month of my activation, and by the end of December 2005, I had written my first spiritual title. In essence, the sixth chakra revealed my purpose in life and what is possible through higher dimensions of consciousness. This has been my unimaginable journey to third eye activation, something I never knew I needed until I directly experienced it.

Post-activation, I have been navigating life in a way that makes sense to me: through compassion and understanding. One hand is rooted in my humanity while the other is extending outwardly into the quantum field and universal consciousness. Every moment is a conscious act of surrender to "what is," because resistance has been laid aside. I approach challenges knowing that an answer or solution is already given. I operate beyond hope. Sixth chakra activation means knowing all is well even when it appears otherwise.

Why I Brought This Book to Life

I wrote this book for two reasons. First, I realized there are many people who are searching for greater self-understanding and want to learn how to tap in to those latent spiritual faculties that have the potential to tremendously improve everyday life. Second, in the last few years I have begun to fully appreciate just how beneficial having enhanced intuition truly is, and I could no longer continue experiencing these psychic events and gifts without sharing them with others.

What you will gain from this book is insight into the chakra system, which will lay the foundation for greater understanding of this often misunderstood and mysterious energy wheel system. From there, the focus will be placed upon the third eye and its massive potential for positive change in your life. This book's insights, meditations, and exercises were developed with one goal in mind: activation of the sixth chakra.

I encourage you to read this book in its entirety before beginning the exercises. Doing so will only enhance your experience during the exercises and better prepare you energetically for the shifts you may experience. After you have finished reading the book, refer back to it often. I have personally found that every time I returned to something, whether it was a book or article, with fresh eyes, insights that were initially overlooked were later revealed in a new light, granting me greater awareness.

A thousand blessings as you begin this extraordinary journey.

chapter one
SIXTH CHAKRA BASICS

The intention for this first chapter is to lay the groundwork and give you a foundation of the chakra system, including the seven chakras found within it. Once we have established a baseline, the focus will then be placed upon the sixth chakra and its profound potential. An activated sixth chakra can open the door to higher dimensions of consciousness and to your psychic abilities and spiritual faculties. Once acknowledged and developed, your abilities and faculties can provide insight and clarity that can be of assistance in virtually every facet of your life.

The chakra system is a group of spinning energy wheels found throughout the subtle body or subtle energy body. Translated from the ancient language of Sanskrit, *chakra* means "wheel." The subtle body is the energy field found in and around your physical body; it is responsible for directing universal energy into the physical body. Through the chakra system, the subtle body functions to maintain physical and emotional health via inner balance of those energy wheels. As your chakras spin, they draw in universal energy and keep the connection between your physical body and the subtle body, your unmanifested aspect.

The Seven Chakras

The seven chakras are as follows, starting at the base of the spine and moving upward: root, sacral, solar plexus, heart, throat, third eye, and crown. Let's now take a closer look at each chakra.

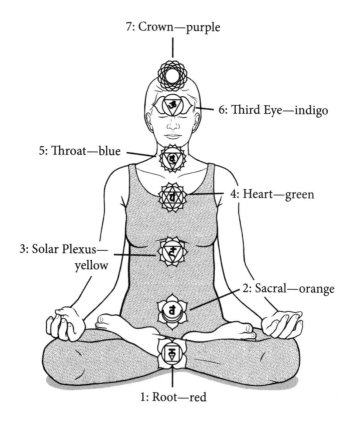

7: Crown—purple

6: Third Eye—indigo

5: Throat—blue

4: Heart—green

3: Solar Plexus—yellow

2: Sacral—orange

1: Root—red

Root Chakra

- **Purpose:** The root chakra serves as your base or foundation.
- **Location:** At the base of the spine. It is the chakra closest to the earth and offers feelings of stability and being grounded.
- **Balanced Chakra:** You feel able to stand on your own and are ready to face challenges.
- **Blocked Chakra:** You experience insecurity and feel like you're on shaky ground.
- **Associated Color:** Red.
- **Positive Affirmation:** "I am secure and able to stand on my own two feet."

Sacral Chakra

- **Purpose:** This chakra is associated with emotions and the ability to express sensuality and creativity.
- **Location:** Just below the navel and above the pubic bone. Passion and playfulness are associated with the sacral chakra.
- **Balanced Chakra:** You can experience nurturing and harmonious relationships.
- **Blocked Chakra:** You have feelings of detachment and low self-esteem.
- **Associated Color:** Orange.
- **Positive Affirmation:** "I am harmonious, and that harmony is reflected in my life and relationships."

Solar Plexus Chakra

- **Purpose:** The solar plexus chakra is characterized by independence and personal power.
- **Location:** In the solar plexus region as the name suggests. Confidence and willpower are reflections of this chakra.
- **Balanced Chakra:** You are open and able to express yourself confidently.
- **Blocked Chakra:** You feel helplessness or experience a lack of direction.
- **Associated Color:** Yellow.
- **Positive Affirmation:** "I am strong and act with courage."

Heart Chakra

- **Purpose:** The center for love and harmony, this chakra enables you to accept yourself and others.
- **Location:** In the center of the chest. It allows you to forgive and extend compassion.
- **Balanced Chakra:** You freely extend love and kindness to those around you.
- **Blocked Chakra:** You tend to hold on to grudges and experience feelings of self-hatred.
- **Associated Color:** Green.
- **Positive Affirmation:** "I am love, and I extend peace and harmony to others."

Throat Chakra

- **Purpose:** The throat chakra allows you to express yourself on a physical and energetic level.
- **Location:** It is located in the neck/throat area. This chakra encourages creativity and authentic self-expression.
- **Balanced Chakra:** You share your highest truths with love and kindness.
- **Blocked Chakra:** You may find it difficult to express yourself. You may feel misunderstood.
- **Associated Color:** Blue.
- **Positive Affirmation:** "I am honest with myself and others."

Third Eye Chakra

- **Purpose:** This is the seat of clarity, wisdom, and intuition. It can also be referred to as the brow or sixth chakra.
- **Location:** In the forehead just between your eyebrows. This chakra is the gateway to your highest self and higher dimensions of consciousness.
- **Balanced Chakra:** You are able to access your inner guidance system consciously.
- **Blocked Chakra:** You find yourself disconnected from your spirituality and experience headaches.
- **Associated Color:** Indigo.
- **Positive Affirmation:** "I am connected to my inner wisdom and intuition."

Crown Chakra

- **Purpose:** The crown chakra represents your connection to your spirituality and highest self.

- **Location:** At the top of the head. This chakra is your connection to universal consciousness.

- **Balanced Chakra:** By operating through an activated third eye, you are able to access higher dimensions of consciousness and awareness.

- **Blocked Chakra:** You are attached to materialism and feel disconnected from universal energy.

- **Associated Color:** Purple.

- **Positive Affirmation:** "I am connected to universal love, now and always."

What an Activated Third Eye Can Do for You

In the introduction, I briefly touched upon just how much my life changed following chakra activation, but I wanted to go further in depth here to discuss the potential and possibilities that lie ahead of you. An activated third eye is a game changer on so many levels. It has the power to literally make tremendous shifts in your life. The first and most important feature of this chakra is its potential to awaken dormant spiritual faculties within you such as clarity, intuition, wisdom, and understanding. Once awakened, these positive spiritual forces can have tremendous and even miraculous effects on your well-being, health, and more.

Clarity is the first gift of an activated third eye. Through clarity, the mind is quieted and relaxed, allowing for your spiritual faculties to flow from Source Energy to your conscious mind with greater reception. Source Energy is the highest self and it has been referred to as spirit, the creator, or a higher power. It is all-encompassing and it is the infinite intelligence, infinite power, and infinite wisdom that is continuously connected with everything and everyone. It is the Source of all life. You can use whatever term you prefer to refer to this higher power. For clarity, I use the term Source or Source Energy. You can read more about these terms in the glossary at the end of the book.

Now, let's get back to clarity. When clarity is achieved, your vibrational frequency will automatically raise, allowing your mind to become a clearer channel for your psychic abilities to express themselves more effectively. With more conscious awareness on your part, you will be empowered and enabled to live more consciously. Everything is energy; vibrational frequency refers to one's energy field. The closer your energy field resonates with Source Energy, the higher your vibrational frequency. On the other hand, vibrations like anger or jealousy lower your vibrational frequency through the density and heaviness of negative emotion. Your psychic abilities will be discussed more in depth later on in this chapter, but I want you to be excited about the possibilities that are awaiting you.

When you become more in tune with wisdom and understanding, you will come into great insight, which gives you a deep understanding of yourself and others. This will have a great impact on your overall well-being because you'll no longer take yourself or others so seriously. It's a win-win all the way around. It allows you to lighten up, figuratively and literally. The other benefit of this increased vibrational frequency is that it can benefit your health as you align more and more with unconditional love and less and less with lower energies like fear or doubt. In other words, a greater flow of energy and communication between Source Energy, the subtle body, and your cells is achieved through clarity, allowing for potential spontaneous healings. This is but a glimpse of the extraordinary potential and possibility of sixth chakra activation.

How to Challenge Negative Thinking

Let's talk about what a negative thought is, why we want to challenge them, and what the practice of challenging negative thinking has to do with the third eye. A negative thought, in essence, is any thought that is based in fear, doubt, sadness, or worry, and it all stems from the conditioned mind, or ego.

Now is as good a time as any to briefly touch upon the ego/conditioned mind because it will be mentioned from time to time. Your ego is the part of you that projects fear and all other negative emotion, plain and simple. Negative thinking leads to negative emotions, which then can lead to self-limiting action or even inaction altogether. The reason we want to challenge negative thinking is because it raises our awareness and empowers us to choose differently. Challenging negative thinking also helps balance your energy; it's the direction toward personal freedom. The ego is the doorman standing between you and third eye activation, which is why it's essential to challenge negative thinking.

How does challenging negative thinking affect the third eye? The third eye is clarity, wisdom, understanding, expanded awareness, and a force that has the potential to silence fear, thereby giving you the ability to clearly feel or sense the wisdom and intuition of your soul. The practice of challenging negative thinking is based in expanded awareness; it puts you in greater alignment with the third eye and brings you closer to its vibrational frequency. You may now be wondering what the vibrational frequency of the third eye is—it's at the frequency of spiritual enlightenment, which we'll get into a little later on in this chapter.

We're going to begin with the first (and probably the most important) exercise on your journey to third eye activation. I'm going to provide you with a simple step-by-step exercise about how to challenge negative thinking. Just keep in mind that to get the most out of every exercise and meditation, you should read the book in its entirety first and then refer back to them. Here we go!

• Challenge Negative Thinking Exercise •

Start by taking fifteen minutes a day to challenge negative thoughts and then build from there as you see fit. This exercise is probably best done at home until you're comfortable with it. If you practice this exercise consistently, you might amaze yourself with just how automatic it can become to challenge negative thinking. Remember, nothing is as difficult as it may seem.

1. The first step is to become aware of your thoughts and the quality of thoughts being offered to you. Are your thoughts disguised as worry, fear, sadness, or regret? Regardless of their form, the goal of negative thoughts is always to create separation, to keep you separated from the truth that you are one with all of life and one with Source Energy. The practice of challenging negative thinking is the beginning of increasing your awareness and expanding your consciousness to sixth chakra level.

2. Next, decide whether or not you're going to believe an automatic negative thought. You see, your belief is what gives life to the energy potential within thoughts. When you believe your automatic thoughts, you are—in essence—making your

conditioned mind or ego-based thinking your reality. And because of that, it's keeping a veil over your spiritual senses and preventing you from becoming aware of them. You will find that as you take back your power by starving fear, worry, or sadness through nonreaction or observation, you will experience greater clarity as you lay aside the limiting thoughts that no longer serve you. Trust me when I say that the power within your consciousness is more than able to withstand and transform any form of negative thinking. In other words, your highest spiritual self doesn't discern one negative thought from another because they are all seen as illusions. As an added bonus, you will also find a greater sense of freedom after choosing to simply observe a negative thought because you are no longer anchored by the past or worried about your future. Rather, you are standing centered and balanced in the present moment, the now, through sixth chakra consciousness. Just to summarize, the second step involves choosing to observe negative thoughts rather than automatically believing or reacting to them.

3. Finally, challenge the negative thought. For example, if you experience the negative thought *I'm feeling stuck*, consciously choose to observe it instead of reacting to it. Then replace it with a positive, conscious thought such as *I am already moving forward in every area of my life*. Notice I used "I am" as I challenged the negative thought. I will discuss the importance of utilizing this phrase, this *command*, in a later chapter.

With practice, you can train yourself to automatically challenge the thoughts or emotions that are preventing you from fully activating the third eye. Each and every time you do so, you are raising your vibrational frequency that much closer to the highest self. You don't have to accept a limited mindset or the consciousness you absorbed while on this planet when you know there is an unlimited awareness available to you through the sixth chakra.

Clair-Everything

We come into this world with these spiritual abilities: clairvoyance, clairaudience, claircognizance, clairsentience, clairgustance, and clairsalience. Some of these you may already be aware of, and some may be more developed than others. Let's take a moment and look at each of these particular abilities individually. These definitions can also be found in the glossary at the end of the book.

- **Clairaudience:** The ability to receive information via psychic auditory means
- **Claircognizance:** The ability to gain knowledge through an inner knowing
- **Clairgustance:** The ability to taste food or another substance without having to put it in your mouth
- **Clairsalience:** The ability to smell an odor/fragrance of a person/place that is not in your immediate surroundings
- **Clairsentience:** Similar to spiritual sonar, this ability allows for information to be received through feelings or emotion; allows for the clear reading of energy

• **Clairvoyance:** The ability to perceive or understand people, objects, or future events through extrasensory perception

Think of these spiritual senses as a spiritual tool chest, each one specifically designed to transcend the limitations of space and time. All of these spiritual senses extend from the third eye, which is always connected to the universal mind and channeled throughout the subtle body as energy, feelings, visions, inner knowing, or intuition. The universal mind has no limits—it is what is all knowing, connected always to everything and everyone.

Looking at these various spiritual gifts, are there any you have consciously experienced? Do any of these abilities come naturally to you? Is there a particular one you would like to further develop and/or master? Remember that desire creates intention, which in turn creates possibility. In other words, anything is possible with enough desire, intention, and action. What I'm trying to say is that we are only limited by the limits we impose upon ourselves. In choosing to go beyond one's perceived limits, we open ourselves up to possibility.

My Claircognizant Moment

One of or many of these spiritual abilities may have become evident at a young age or may present itself later in life. A psychic ability or event may also be experienced spontaneously when it matters the most, like when urgency or white-hot desire is experienced. Let me give you an example.

Many years ago, I was studying to become a dental hygienist in Ohio. The college I attended was over four hundred miles from my hometown, where my girlfriend at the time still lived because she was in her last year of high school. One day, in my first few weeks of starting my curriculum, I received a frantic phone call from my girlfriend. She told me a stranger had tried talking to her as she walked to school. After ignoring his advancements, he ended up chasing her all the way to the doors of the high school. This news rocked me to my core and left me feeling helpless because I was so far away.

Weeks went by and my girlfriend started receiving prank phone calls from this individual. Understandably, she was starting to become afraid to leave the house. The calls got so frequent that the police got involved and started tracing the phone calls. By this time, I was making the trek back home on the weekends to try to comfort her and, if possible, to help the police find this individual.

About a month into the situation, the authorities told my girlfriend which local intersection they had traced the calls to. I was in my apartment in Ohio when my girlfriend called me midweek just to tell me that the police had found the area the calls were coming from. Fearing I would go out, find, and confront this person if I had this newly acquired knowledge, she refused to tell me which intersection it was.

In a brief moment of what I would describe as an emotional charge or buildup, I experienced profound insight. The name of the intersection came to me in a vision in my mind's eye. "Barton and Lottridge!" I suddenly shouted.

My girlfriend, stunned by what I had just said, went silent for a few seconds. Then she asked, "How did you know?"

"It just came to me in a vision," I said.

But knowing the intersection wasn't enough information to catch the man making those harassing phone calls, because he didn't even live in that area. He was going there just to make those harassing phone calls. He might never have been located if not for my girlfriend's mother and a twist of fate.

One day shortly after the calls had been successfully traced, my girlfriend's mother went on a walk not far from their home. As she approached a commercial building with an apartment overhead, she saw an individual standing on the balcony. Instantly, she knew she had found the man making the harassing calls; there was no doubt in her mind. When she got home, she told her daughter, who then informed me of his whereabouts.

Thankfully, I was in town. I decided to head over to his apartment. When I arrived, he was still on the balcony. I instantly knew that he was the guy I was looking for. I got out of my vehicle and approached the building. As I looked up, I saw the shock and terror in his eyes. I stopped just below the balcony and—feeling a surge of energy I don't think I had ever experienced before—advised him, in no uncertain terms, to leave my girlfriend alone. The entire time I spoke to him, he did not utter a word.

A few days later, I followed up with the apartment's landlord and found out that the tenant had suddenly moved out. And thankfully, the phone calls and drama all subsided and my girlfriend was able to once again be her happy-go-lucky self.

Looking back, there was no other way I could have known where the phone calls were coming from except by psychic means. I was several hundred miles away. My girlfriend refused to tell me the intersection. And by the way, that intersection had not been on my radar in the slightest because it was over a mile from her house.

The point of this story was to show you that these spiritual gifts are already encoded within us; they don't have to be attained. They can express themselves through desire and intention. I also wanted to hammer home the notion that time and space are inconsequential when tapping in to higher dimensions of consciousness because in the spiritual realm, they do not exist—all is here and now. With all of that being said, your spiritual abilities can be further developed and mastered through chakra activation, which enhances your awareness of them, thereby strengthening your connection to them. Lastly, through the clarity of the third eye, insights, wisdom, and knowledge can more easily be accessed through the state of allowing or a vibration of nonresistance.

Spiritual Sonar

Many of us—if not all of us—have experienced hunches or moments of intuition. We've all heard of people who have averted disaster when they've listened to their intuition. The goal here is to give you a hyperawareness of that intuition the next time it comes into play. This brings us to the power of focus. The conditioned mind likes to drift between past and future; it just does this. And to be frank, it is what it is; it's not good or bad for your mind to drift. It's just the contrast to who you really are: a spiritual, present-based being. The universal mind, however, is one with the third eye; that is where your intuition, wisdom, and clarity are found.

There is a tremendous amount of information in the space around you, just waiting for you to become fully aware of it so that it can be accessed. Everything in life is a mirror, and when you look upon and focus on the "nothingness" around you, it will begin to reflect clarity back to you. Clarity abounds in the universe; it has the power to begin to still or quiet your mind because it is flowing from the sixth chakra always. However, clarity often goes unrecognized due to the distraction of thoughts and emotions. Every time you expand the gap of nothingness or stillness between your thoughts, you come one step closer to allowing the third eye to blossom and activate. The quieter the mind becomes, the more still you become, and the more you are in a state of allowing, which opens the door to clarity, wisdom, and potentially mystical experiences.

Now that I have given you some background, let's talk more about spiritual sonar. It's usually described as *clairsentience*, but I find that the term *spiritual sonar* is more direct and to the point. As mentioned earlier, everything is energy, seen and unseen. There's a lot going on in the nothingness. We are all connected via telepathy; the best way to describe it would be that we are all tied to invisible energy circuits which are pathways of information. When you are focused and aligned with sixth chakra consciousness, you can penetrate through the veil and read and decipher energetically what is before you, regardless of distance.

On a conscious level, you can apply spiritual sonar through intention, imagining or willing waves of energy to release from your inner being and allowing that energy to return to you with information in the form of vibrations or feelings. This is a conscious and active approach to clairsentience. As you become more present and more focused regardless of where you are, be it a busy shopping mall or grocery store, these places will have less of an impact on your ability to perceive and read energy information. I used to apply spiritual sonar without fully realizing it when I worked as undercover store security after high school; I would linger near the front of the store and send out energy as people came in. In return, I would receive information energetically about who was going to shoplift, and this information had great accuracy.

Let's do a simple exercise on spiritual sonar development. The goal is to improve your focus and to allow energetic information to be received and understood through greater clarity. This exercise can be done almost anywhere: a mall, a store, etc. The noisier the better! I want you to be able to train yourself to be present and focused regardless of what's around you. This, in other words, is an exercise of going inward and listening, feeling, seeing, reading, and paying attention.

• Spiritual Sonar Exercise •

Start by practicing this exercise in ten-to-fifteen-minute intervals and work your way up. Place yourself in a mall or go for a walk outside; make sure there are people around you.

1. Bring your awareness to the here and now. In other words, become very present.

2. For the first minute or two, bring your awareness and focus to the third eye area. Become aware of it and allow anything that attempts to distract you to come and go. Remain focused and relaxed. Less effort is more when it comes to spiritual practice.

3. Once your energy is focused, start imagining waves of energy emanating from you like invisible ripples. As you're doing this, continue to pay attention to the energy in and around you because the information can come quite fast. Pay close attention to any feelings you may be picking up on. In other words, allow the information to be received. Perhaps you would like to try placing your attention on a group of people to see what information returns. This is the kind of information you might receive while doing this: You may feel energetically that one or two people in the group are going to decide to split from the rest of the group

before it actually happens. You might pick up on their spirit guides or a loved one who has passed. You might get a sense of their feelings or emotions. Regardless, keep the information to yourself, keeping in mind that this is practice. It is simply an exercise in developing your ability to read energy in your environment and the people around you. Once you've done this for about ten minutes, it's time to end the exercise.

4. Bring your awareness back. Take a deep breath and let the experience go until next time.

Once you've mastered this exercise, spiritual sonar can happen or take place quite spontaneously, especially when it's most needed. Remember that these abilities are expressions of the soul—energy, vibration, and feeling are its language.

On a final note, this ability has been quite useful in my everyday life. It gives me a greater understanding of the world around me, allowing me to be in tune with my environment.

chapter two
SPIRITUAL FOUNDATIONS

Because an activated third eye is responsible for clarity by clearing negative thoughts from your consciousness, it also acts as the faucet for energy flow throughout the physical and subtle energy body. It accomplishes this by elevating your awareness or consciousness to the point where negative energies—like fear, for example—cannot reach those heights. As your awareness increases, higher dimensions of consciousness become available. And one of the keys to experiencing these higher dimensions is a deep awareness of the present moment, the now.

The Importance of the Now

Reflect on the following: The past often comes with sadness, regret, and attachment. The future usually offers fear or some form of worry. The present moment, however, offers you this: an emotional elevator and a sense of greater freedom. And by freedom,

I mean a way for you to raise your consciousness up from the lower-vibrating energies and emotions that are blocking your energy from flowing freely. It would seem, then, that living with present moment awareness is one of the first steps to clearing up your vibrational frequency, allowing for the blossoming of the third eye.

Through the present moment, your conscious mind comes into closer alignment with your authentic spiritual self, the soul. And by becoming more aligned with spirit, you begin to soften the walls separating you from the highest self, allowing for the flow of wisdom from the universal mind to your local, conscious mind. All of this starts a domino effect, spiritually speaking, because with the flow of wisdom comes inspired action. And each action you take toward activating the sixth chakra leads you to another action and then another, each time building momentum and eventually leading you to an inner shift, a shift from third-dimensional consciousness to universal consciousness, unbound awareness, which is in fact your natural state of being.

Since the sixth chakra is based in the nonphysical or unmanifested world, the majority of focus will be on what you can do energetically to clear up your energy field to prepare for its activation. To be clear, the third eye is the juxtaposition where your awareness and Source Energy merge, which allows for a clear line for instant communication. With a clear channel, you are able to receive direction and even warnings from your spirit guides, read into the past and future because it's all happening in the now, and pierce through to the truth of a situation, seeing beyond any veil of deception. To further clarify, the third eye is your way of seeing and experiencing life through oneness via your spiritual self. And because there ultimately is no time and space in these higher spiritual dimensions, information is literally available faster than the speed of light.

Operating from the sixth chakra through the present moment will also bring a lightness to the body due to the shedding of old emotions or limiting beliefs. Looking back, I remember saying to my brother-in-law Gabe shortly after my chakra activated, "I feel like a rag doll, there's such lightness to my arms." Keep in mind that aligning with this elevated awareness is not as difficult as it seems; one of the key ingredients is simply being aware of the present moment.

Doorway to Enlightenment

We'll be looking at elevated awareness more in depth in a later chapter, but I felt it necessary to lay a preliminary foundation here because it's so closely tied with the third eye. What I'm going to offer you in this section is an initial overview of how enlightenment and the third eye mirror each other. Let's take a look at this light-filled state.

If enlightenment is the door, then the third eye is the key that unlocks it. In other words, an activated sixth chakra clears one's energy field and leads to knowing, sensing, and understanding, just to name a few spiritual faculties that come to life in this awareness. Think of the third eye as a light switch; the light—enlightenment—reveals insight, greater intuition, and self-understanding. Here's a simple and straightforward definition of enlightenment: it's an acknowledgment and direct experience of your inner being, the spirit within you, your unmanifested self; you could also describe it as spiritual alignment. And it's the profound awareness of the reality of oneness that again is based in the channel that is sixth chakra consciousness. Through an activated third eye you not only experience clarity and wisdom, you become it. The veil of this world is pierced and you, in essence, are operating consciously from expanded awareness, an awareness of the spiritual realm.

Through this elevated awareness you're able to access many other spiritual faculties, including abilities you weren't even aware of. Enlightenment is an evolutionary step, a forward step in consciousnesses. This is why you can't help but evolve and grow as you fulfill the desire to activate the sixth chakra and master your psychic abilities. All of it is tied together. The clearer the channel, the greater the wisdom you have. The more aware you are, the greater the possibilities. The greater the possibilities, the more limitless your potential, and so on.

Ultimately, enlightenment is a conscious balancing act of the thoughts and emotions within your energy field. It's achieved by observing rather than reacting to them, including the practice of challenging negative thinking. This inner balance clears the way for your inner being to express itself as joy, peace, clarity, happiness, and abilities beyond the five senses. Enlightenment is also a process—a continuous process—of letting go of the things that are always attempting to block you energetically, namely negative emotions.

Third eye activation and enlightenment go hand in hand. If you're seeking enlightenment, then you're looking to activate the third eye. If you're trying to activate the third eye, then you're going to experience enlightenment. It's that simple. They are reflections of each other; the third eye is the channel and the station received is expanded awareness, the state of enlightenment.

As we move forward, I want you to be mindful that all of the exercises, practices, wisdom, examples, and personal experiences in this book are given with one single goal in mind: to assist you in creating the perfect condition within yourself to experience gradual or spontaneous third eye activation. As we continue on this journey, you will discover more ways to raise your vibrational frequency, thereby better aligning yourself with sixth chakra consciousness and the psychic abilities that are reflected through it.

Tuning In to Higher Dimensions

Almost everyone has experienced aha moments or moments of clarity that have directed and guided them, usually in a time of need. If you have had one of these extraordinary moments, you did so by temporarily raising your own frequency vibration through intense desire for an answer, which then allowed you to access higher dimensions of wisdom or guidance through the sixth chakra. Some would describe these moments as a stroke of genius. My point here is to not only make you aware that it's happened for you in the past, but to show you how to access those higher frequencies more often and with greater conscious awareness.

This practice requires discernment on your part and a desire or willingness to consciously tune in to the higher dimensions of consciousness within you. Let us begin by discussing the topic of discernment, which requires you to place your attention inward. What you're going to be focusing on is the still, small voice of wisdom emanating from your highest self. Wisdom and guidance are always being offered to us, but for many, they're often neglected or overshadowed by thoughts and emotions from another source, the ego. This is how you can tell the difference between information coming from the sixth chakra channel and that of the ego: The information coming from higher dimensions will have clarity to it and a feeling of unconditional love that is without fear, uncertainty, or doubt. In other words, it will have a higher vibration to it. On the other hand, ego-sponsored thoughts will come as fear disguised in a variety of forms such as doubt, uncertainty, and anger, all of which are low-vibrating energies. Like anything else, practice makes perfect; spending several minutes a day in a quiet room focused on receiving higher-dimensional information and learning to recognize it will help you open up the channel for greater clarity and wisdom.

Let's move on to tuning in to higher dimensions of consciousness. Most of us do this every day with little or no conscious awareness, and that's because third-dimensional reality is so seductive and persistent. You're experiencing higher frequencies every time you come into alignment with feelings of appreciation or gratitude. It happens whenever you extend kindness to a stranger. These feelings—like appreciation, gratitude, and kindness—are all extensions of unconditional love, the highest vibration there is. And when you are in that space, you are in fact expressing Source Energy through you. Now you must become more aware of it. I've said it before and I'll say it again: Awareness is everything. What you are aware of is what is made manifest in your reality.

There are other high-vibrating feelings you can express, and you don't have to wait for a circumstance or a change to experience them. Happiness is a choice. Thinking or saying "I am happy" throughout the day, without attaching that phrase to anything, is incredibly high-frequency based. Practicing quiet or silent meditations where you focus on nothingness or inner stillness produces wonderful results in raising your vibrational frequency through the brow chakra, allowing higher-dimensional access, but that will be further discussed in the next chapter.

And so, with the background given, let's look at an exercise for creating greater discernment while tuning in to higher dimensions of consciousness.

Discernment and Tuning In to Higher Dimensions Exercise

1. Choose a quiet space and get comfortable.

2. Take a few deep breaths and relax your shoulders. Your eyes can be open or closed.

3. Focus on the awareness of the present moment.

4. After a minute or two of anchoring yourself in the present, bring your attention inward.

5. Bring your awareness to your thoughts. Don't judge them; observe them, be witness to them. Do this for five minutes.

6. Bring your awareness a little deeper, to the gap between your thoughts. That is where the soul speaks to you. Ask a question if you feel inspired to do so, such as "Who are my spirit guides?" Feel free to inquire for another minute or two. Continue to pay attention; wisdom and guidance will be offered by that still, soft voice within you.

7. For the next two minutes, think of high-vibrating feelings. Choose thoughts that tune you in to higher dimensions of consciousness such as happiness and gratitude. Say, "I am happy." Smile and feel the emotion as you express it. Repeat this phrase two or three times. Then say, "I am grateful for this gift called life." Repeat this phrase two or three times. Feel the gratitude within you; feel the shift in consciousness.

8. When you're done, take a few deep breaths and return your awareness to the surface. Then let the moment go. Give thanks once more.

This exercise can be done once or twice a week, gradually increasing how often you practice this exercise.

From Belief to Knowing

The shift from third-dimensional to sixth chakra consciousness takes you from belief to knowing. Keep in mind that one level of awareness is not superior to another; rather, different points of view or perception are experienced because we live in a world of contrast, or so it seems on the surface. Another thing to note is that each individual soul is experiencing their journey to ascension on their own evolutionary schedule. Being the "seat of the soul," the third eye is clear knowing in and of itself; it's a direct channel to divine wisdom and understanding. When old limiting beliefs collide with knowing, it's like when a subcompact car drives into an eighteen-wheeler; the belief will crash and break apart against the weight and strength of knowing because knowing is immovable, not apt to change—it simply is. Knowing doesn't require any further explanation because the truth is experienced directly through the third eye. Clarity is directly experienced through stillness. And through clarity, massive amounts of wisdom and information are downloaded from universal to individual consciousness. Wisdom, then, would appear to be a one-way street from the highest self to the local self.

The following insights—combined with your awareness of them—are one way that you can begin to make the shift from belief to knowing, thereby moving energetically closer to the third eye and its activation. Aligning with these powerful truths and realizing that they are coming from higher dimensions gives them transformative power when one resonates with their frequency. Reflect on these spiritual realm offerings:

- You are a powerful, creative, spiritual being able to manifest your reality through thoughts, emotions, words, and deeds. Everything about you is creative.

- Thoughts and words are doorways to alternate realities. In other words, your beliefs shape your personal reality. Thoughts are powerful, but words have even more energy behind them.

- You came into this world already equipped with every spiritual tool and faculty you could need to fulfill your purpose and be successful in this life.

- Fear has been misinterpreted and allowed to grow on this planet. It was always meant to be a catalyst for transformation, for you cannot know who and what you are until you experience what you are not.

- Your desires and intentions are powerful. Dream bigger. Come from the space of awareness that your dreams are in fact already fulfilled; gratitude and appreciation are the keys to manifesting what you desire.

- Remember to engage and develop these two life-changing spiritual forces: faith and trust.

- You are always guided and surrounded by angels. You just have to call upon them.

- You are one with everything and everyone; everything and everyone are a part of you. Therefore, see all as one.

- Forgiveness leads to greater clarity because it releases you from the past and all of the guilt associated with it. Therefore, forgive those who need your forgiveness, because in doing so you are only forgiving yourself.

- You do not need to seek peace anywhere outside of yourself. It is found and experienced through the channel of the sixth chakra as inner stillness.
- Meditation is everything.
- Let go of the things that no longer serve you, which are weighing you down. Love yourself enough to let go.

All you have to do is reflect and meditate upon these words if they ring true to you. It's interesting—I have found that as I focus my attention on high-vibrating thoughts, others seem to follow, and the next thing I know I am expanding my awareness and consciousness even further. The body may have limits, but there are none to the mind. There is no limit to what you can become.

Reflect on these insights as you feel necessary. With that being said, take these twelve insights and develop your own, then use them as your own personal mantras. Once you've created your own, refer to them just for a few minutes weekly and allow them to resonate within you and raise your vibrational frequency. Let's get started!

• Self-Empowering Mantras Activity •

1. Reflect on the insights I've offered and allow yourself to resonate with them for a few minutes. Then take what feels right and true for you and expand. Come from a place of potential; anything is possible.

2. Take a pen and pad of paper and allow inspiration to guide you as you ask yourself this question: What is true for me now?

Spend ten or fifteen minutes brainstorming and writing down new and empowering mantras, mantras that uplift, elevate, and feel absolutely wonderful. Allow yourself to be inspired. These new mantras—these new inner truths—have the potential to lead you to greater insights and higher-vibrational frequencies; they are that powerful.

chapter three

WHO ARE YOU?
INSIGHTS THAT ELEVATE

This chapter is going to be all about insights that will increase your awareness and point you inward so that you can realize who you are on a spiritual level. Being in alignment with your spiritual self is essential because through your authentic self, intuition becomes clearer. Knowing who you are on a deeper level can help you find your purpose, give you direction, and reveal to you just what is possible. These insights and exercises will bring you closer to mind, body, and spiritual alignment.

Awareness is what brings things to life and into your experience. Inner stillness is a reflection of your inner being, which is your spiritual self. It's a state of mind free of thought and negative emotion. Some describe it as an empty mind, but there is a lot of potential in that nothingness. Through that inner quiet, one can tune in to wisdom and understanding or be guided by a spiritual guide. It is also the universal frequency of the universe, the mind of Source Energy, and everything emanates from it—yes, everything is coming from nothing. Inner stillness is a reality rooted in the present; however, it can be overlooked by remaining and keeping your awareness strictly within the confines of the conditioned mind or third-dimensional consciousness, which, again, tends to operate between the past and future instead of in the now.

Inner stillness is the channel of the third eye, and it's the direct link to clarity and wisdom as well as the door to experiencing inner peace and understanding. In other words, it's the awareness that offers you a peek behind the veil to all the unseen inner workings of life itself. It's also the field of limitless potential and where all your psychic abilities will be found. In essence, it's clarity that reveals your highest self, who you are beyond the thinking mind.

Words are powerful and have a lot of potential within them. And when words are emanating from higher dimensions of consciousness, they are transformative in nature because they are higher in frequency, more soul-based. Because of that, they can potentially elevate your awareness, making it easier for you to let go of any limiting ideas you may have had about who you really are. These are potentials waiting to be experienced through the insight of the third eye: the reality of higher dimensions of consciousness and the power to really change your life through an activated sixth chakra.

Inner stillness is the song of the universe and its melody is oneness. Oneness is what is directly experienced in spiritual reality. It's the higher spiritual awareness that reveals everything and everyone is unified. Stillness, then, is the song or vibrational frequency, the unifying energy that points you to who and what you are.

A few tips on inner stillness: Meditate upon it when you can, allowing it to come to the forefront of your consciousness more often. As you allow inner stillness to come into your awareness, you also are allowing the third eye to mature so that it can ultimately fully bloom through activation. In other words, practice inner silence. It's interesting—the more you let go in terms of the past and limiting beliefs, the more complete and whole you'll realize you already are. And the more you let go, the more your consciousness will expand. In other words, when you empty yourself, you make room for the universe to pour in wisdom, abundance, health, happiness, joy, and more.

Now that you've been introduced to inner stillness and its relevance to the third eye, let's move into a meditation that is designed with the intention to raise your awareness to higher dimensions of consciousness and the potentiality of the third eye.

• Inner Stillness Meditation •

1. Get into a comfortable meditation position. Preferably, your spine is straight, your head is erect, and you are relaxed and in a state of allowing. Your eyes can be open or closed. Follow your breaths for a few moments, allowing for deeper relaxation.

2. Bring your attention inward and observe what comes to you without judgment. In other words, become aware of your thoughts. After a minute or two, bring your attention to the gaps or spaces of nothingness between your thoughts. That gap of nothingness is the very essence of your inner being; it is stillness. Bring your focus to the stillness, the silence that is ever present within you. Spend five minutes doing this.

3. If your eyes have been closed, open them and become aware of the space, the nothingness, all around you. If there is a plant in your room, focus on the plant and recognize the stillness of it. Let that nothingness be reflected in you. Realize that stillness is found everywhere and in all things. Continue with this for ten or fifteen minutes.

4. As you're meditating, become aware of the energy in and around your physical body. You may find that you can begin to feel the subtle energy body as your vibrational frequency increases during this practice; it is felt as waves of energy.

5. At the end of your meditation practice, take a deep breath and let go of the moment with gratitude.

This meditative practice can be quite elevating and transformative. Tuning your vibrational frequency to inner stillness should be greatly desired because it's the channel of sixth chakra consciousness. It's the field of consciousness where you will find clarity, wisdom, understanding, and your psychic abilities. In other words, it's the frequency of enlightenment.

Wakeful Meditation

Wakeful meditation is the practice of being present and centered through inner stillness as you go about your day. It may sound a little daunting, but it's the reality you'll experience when you operate from sixth chakra consciousness or higher dimensions. This is what wakeful meditation look likes: You're washing dishes, present and aware in the knowing that you're washing dishes and nothing more. You're at the movies, present and aware in the knowing that you're at the movies and nothing more. You're spending time with a friend, present and aware in the knowing that you're doing just that and nothing more. The benefits of being in this state of awareness are too many to mention, but I'll give you a few: elevated awareness, higher vibrational frequency, and greater clarity. If I were to describe this state in two words, while offering insight as to how to achieve this moment-by-moment way of living, it would be this: expanded awareness.

Here are some pointers or things to be mindful of as you invite inner stillness into your awareness so that you may better align yourself with the frequency of the third eye.

Wakeful Meditation Pointers

- Wherever you are, just be present. Be present in your body. In other words, focus on what's in front of you while you're aware of what's within you, mainly inner stillness.

- Be aware of your breaths. The exhale and inhale, the coming and going—this is a great way to become very aware of each moment.

- Remember to relax. Be mindful of your posture. A relaxed mind is more receptive to intuition.

- Become more aware of stillness: the stillness between spoken words, the stillness around you. What about the space of "nothingness" between these letters? In other words, start recognizing the nothingness and how it makes the manifested things in this world possible.

- Immerse yourself in whatever you're doing. Really feel the pen you're holding or the keyboard you're striking with your fingers. Feel the aliveness within you.

- Remember not to take yourself or others too seriously.

- You can't think your way to inner stillness—you can only become aware of it via relaxation and meditative practice through letting go.

- The next person you encounter or the next billboard you see may have something to offer you; it might be a message. Expand your awareness to this possibility.

- Look for the beauty in your moments by realizing the fleetingness of them.

- Be mindful that there is tremendous potential and possibility in every moment.

Clarity through Insight

I'm going to offer you a simple exercise that has the potential to activate the eye of clarity. This exercise will bring greater awareness to the thoughts and emotions being offered to you from the ego, which will enable you to look at them with greater clarity, discernment, and insight. I call this exercise the Eye of Clarity Exercise.

• Eye of Clarity Exercise •

1. Start with a piece of blank paper and a pen.

2. Write down the thoughts coming to you for a minute or two.

3. After you've spent a minute or two writing down these thoughts and emotions, take another minute or two and look at the thoughts. Can you identify the emotions surrounding these thoughts? Are they fearful? Are they filled with doubt? Are they from the past? Are they projecting

into the future? Is there sadness to them? Is there worry within them? Are they negative? Are they distracting to the present moment? Clear your mind and really look at these thoughts and emotions. Ask yourself if they're serving you. Ask yourself if they are empowering you.

4. Perform this exercise once or twice daily; it only takes five minutes each time. Know that the moment you begin to question what thoughts are coming to mind is the moment you're bringing greater awareness into the picture. The moment you start to challenge any automatic negative thoughts is the instant you've entered the atmosphere of potential, inviting its friend, possibility.

Intuition Speaks Always

We're always being spiritually guided, from the smallest choices to the largest decisions. Nothing is unimportant to our spiritual guides—or to Source Energy, for that matter. We have to be aware of the countless ways that messages are being offered. Remember that spiritual guidance is not a transitory thing; one can be attuned to the highest self quite often and even reach the point where it's just a part of everyday life.

Your spirit guides and your highest self have a great interest in you and your daily life. They love you unconditionally and adore you, so these higher-dimensional beings always have your best interest at heart. If you've been thinking that some issues or problems you're facing are somehow beneath them, think again. Answers and elevated perspectives are waiting for you; you just need to decide to get meditative and tune in to divine wisdom and guidance. You're never without help or assistance. Tune in, ask a question, or share your dilemma with your spirit guides.

Then listen—actively listen. You might just be amazed at what comes to you.

The universe can choose to communicate with you in many ways; perhaps there is a message in the next fortune cookie you open, the next article you read, or the next phrase you hear on the radio. You see, the universe is always—and I mean always—speaking to us, but the question is, who's listening? We improve our listening skills, spiritually speaking, by becoming more aware and more attentive to our inner world of thought through present moment awareness. Greater awareness leads to greater discernment, and living more presently slows down the stream of automatic thought, making room for clarity to arise. And through clarity, hearing the still, small voice of intuition becomes easier, making higher-dimensional wisdom a more effortless experience.

You may have noticed by now that awareness is a building process. Being aware of one thing opens the door to more awareness and so on. Just as there's no limit to consciousness, there's no limit to what you can be made aware of. As one level of understanding is reached, another is waiting to be understood. Welcome wisdom and understanding on a daily basis. You welcome wisdom and understanding whenever you're in a space of nonresistance. You invite wisdom and understanding whenever you're meditating and raising your vibrational frequency. You encourage higher-dimensional guidance whenever you're feeling appreciation and gratitude. All of these actions are energy raising and make guidance more easily recognized and more frequently experienced. You already have the radio, you just have to set the dial to 101 Wisdom FM, so to speak.

Intuition Insights

- Intuition is always being offered energetically through feelings and vibrations.

- Awareness and attentiveness lead to perceptiveness.

- Everything is potentially information.

- The more you recognize it, the more evident intuition becomes.

- As you become more in tune with universal consciousness and inner stillness, you will experience greater clarity, making it easier to interpret energy.

- There are several ways the universe gets its messages across.

- Clarity is only a frequency away; tune in to it.

- Intuition is a part of your inner being, an expression of it.

Synchronicity and You

We're going to take a closer look at synchronicity because the more you recognize it in your life, the more you can connect the dots and realize that you are in fact cocreating with the universe. You are a unique and important part of the universe, an expression of Source Energy. As your energy shifts more toward third eye awareness, you will become more aware of the interconnectedness of everything, including the events in your life. When you think of the word *synchronicity*, what comes to mind? Do events in your life seem orchestrated or simply random? I consider synchronicities to be little miracles from the universe reminding me that I'm supported and cared for by my highest self as I move forward in my life. These little miracles may come as encounters with the right person at the right time or an unexpected opportunity, but there are countless possibilities for how synchronicities will express themselves for you.

When it comes to synchronicity, it all comes down to this: Pay attention to the signs and their meanings. If you can recognize the signs and see the message within them, then you can follow and act upon them. How will you know when to act upon a synchronicity? Pay attention to how you feel; feel the energy of the synchronistic event and allow that to resonate within you. Does it feel good? Is there a flow to it? Or do you feel caution, like this may not be for you? You see, synchronicity operates through your awareness and inner guidance system. Good feelings and not-so-good feelings are at play here, and for good reason. For example, let's say you're out car shopping and you're about to sign the papers, but you get a feeling in the pit of your stomach that something's just not right. If you have a not-so-good feeling about something, don't fret over it. Pay attention to the feeling and honor it; it's just one of the ways that the universe is communicating with you. If something doesn't feel right, walk away. And remember, you can always choose to be confident that something better is on the horizon.

Expanding your awareness to the reality of synchronicity is an exercise in aligning your energy with that of the third eye's intuitive nature. The following list offers pointers to assist you with opening up to synchronicities in order to experience the fullness of them.

Ten Ways to Recognize Synchronicity

1. Know that you are supported and cared for. The universe is unconditional love, and that love is always being extended to you in countless ways, including synchronicity.

2. Become more aware of synchronicity. Acknowledge it. It is always in effect.

3. Look for the meaning behind a synchronicity. When you look deeper into that chance encounter or opportunity, you are peeking behind the veil, which leads to insight.

4. Don't second-guess things. Instead, honor your feelings by trusting your intuitive nature more.

5. Take action. Follow up synchronicities with the necessary steps by listening and paying attention to your inner guidance system.

6. See others as a part of the universe. The next step in your life may reveal itself via a conversation with a friend or even a stranger in the grocery store.

7. Pay attention to number sequences like 1111 or 444. If you see these numbers often, it is a reminder that you are being guided. The sequence 1111 refers to your alignment or oneness with the universe. The sequence 444 reminds you to stay connected with your intuition and inner guidance.

8. Look back using retrocognition or spiritual hindsight. Briefly look at the events of the past week, month, or year. Can you see where some events seem more than just coincidences? Is it apparent how some decisions led you to certain moments in time where you received just what you needed, when you needed it?

9. Pay attention to the sense that something is about to happen. Perhaps you are thinking about making a phone call to a loved one and then they call you. This kind of phenomena is a manifestation of your psychic abilities and shows how they tie in with synchronicity.

10. Trust the feeling that you're following your path. If things are easily falling into place, this is a universal nod, saying, "Yes, you're in the flow!"

Cause and Effect

In this section we're going to look at cause and effect and how you can make the shift to consciously manifesting your life instead of being at the whim of the effects or circumstances in your life. By operating from the cause point of view, you'll claim responsibility for your life and by doing so, reclaim your vital energy and power. Not only that, but as you think consciously you will become more aligned with third eye consciousness, which is that higher frequency and understanding that thoughts and emotions can become things.

The universal law for cause and effect represents that for every effect or circumstance there is a cause or source. You can approach life from the cause or effect point of view. If you approach life from the effect side of things, you are left reacting to thoughts, emotions, and circumstances. This approach can leave you feeling somewhat helpless at times because there is a sense that you can't help what you're feeling or where you are in your life. When things are going great, you feel great! When things aren't going so hot, that tends to reflect in the way you feel. Now, there's nothing wrong with this way of being. However, the question is, is this way of being still serving you?

Operating from the cause point of view allows you to reclaim your energy by realizing you are manifesting your reality through thoughts, emotions, and expectations. You are the cause of your experiences. If you operate from this point of view, you can center yourself in the knowing that you can redirect your energy.

You can choose not to focus and spend all your energy thinking about or focusing on the effects. Instead, you can set new intentions. Because you can change your vibrational frequency, you can change your thoughts, emotions, and circumstances. By deciding what you desire out of life, you can become a person who consciously manifests their reality by choosing different thoughts and emotions.

The following are examples of conscious thinking that can help you become more focused and centered in your being, laying the groundwork for you to become more conscious of how you approach your life. These simple yet powerful phrases can be repeated a few times a day.

Cause and Effect Insights

- "I am manifesting my reality through greater awareness, and I am free to choose differently."
- "My intention is to be aligned with the third eye and its awareness."
- "I reclaim my vital energy and power now."
- "By accepting what is, I am no longer resisting it. Therefore, I can change it."
- "I am open to becoming a channel for greater intuition and wisdom."
- "There is nothing but potential and possibility in my life."
- "I am free to change the direction of my life."
- "Effects are only a reflection of past thinking, and I can change my pattern of thought."

Your Inner Being

Becoming aware of and understanding who you are at the spiritual level elevates you and gives you greater insight to who you are beyond the physical body. By knowing who you are spiritually, you can then get a better sense of your place in this big, beautiful universe.

Your inner being is your awareness—it's you. It's that quiet awareness, that part of you that simply knows. And it's always in contact with Source Energy. There, you've been introduced. Now say hello to your soul. Your soul is understanding and clarity. It is unconditional love and joy. It is freedom and peace, and there is nothing complicated about that.

Your inner being has one desire, and that's to be remembered. That is, to be rejoined consciously so that you can live your best life, the life of your dreams. This is important because of where we're headed in the next chapter. With that being said, I'm going to provide you with ten ways to get in touch with your inner being—the soul—so that you can shift and align yourself with its unconditional love, wisdom, and intuition.

Ten Ways to Get in Touch with Your Inner Being

1. Find silence through meditative practice, even for just a few minutes a day.

2. Be of service to others. Try volunteering or being a mentor.

3. Reconnect with nature.

4. Travel. It has a way of resetting us and providing a fresh start.

5. Ask your inner being to reveal itself.

6. Become more aware of the energy within you and around you.

7. Focus on your breathing for a few minutes a day.

8. Do things that bring out the joy in you.

9. Practice patience, with yourself and others.

10. Be compassionate. Compassion is a direct reflection of unconditional love, and to be in this space is to be one with the soul.

chapter four

INTENTION LEADS TO
CLEAR FOCUS

This chapter focuses on inner clarity so that this essential, spiritual attribute can help guide you in your everyday life and in your decision-making. Clarity, in all its facets, is the foundation to building a successful spiritual life and being able to access your psychic abilities. We're going to start with clarity of mind and how it's then reflected in physical aspects as you consciously merge with your spiritual aspect.

The first step in experiencing clarity of mind is to know what the desired result is. That's called setting your intention, which, in this case, is a calm and relaxed state of mind. In other words, you want to become mindful of your spiritual aspect so that your spirit's clarity and peace can be reflected in your mind. It's your focused awareness that leads you to experience confusion or clarity, doubt or certainty. Shifting your attention inward toward your inner being is how to achieve the inner clarity I'm talking about. And at the end of this section, I will offer you tips and an exercise on becoming clear in all three aspects of your being.

Back to getting into a calm and relaxed state of mind—this state of mind has its awareness anchored in the present while still being consciously aware of thoughts of the past and future that tend to arise. In other words, letting the past be where it should be—the past—while consciously choosing your intentions for the future is what invites greater clarity. This approach clears the mind, allowing for the potential of the present to speak to you. And by setting future intentions on a conscious level, you open the door to a better and brighter future by overriding what the conditioned mind is trying to dictate to you.

Here are some examples of intentions that you can choose to think and speak to shift you closer toward clarity of mind:

- "I am clear and focused."
- "I am calm and relaxed in the knowing that my life is unfolding perfectly."
- "I am aware of my potential to create consciously through the present."
- "My mind is a reflection of my inner being."
- "I am at peace with what is as I reach for greater awareness and new experiences."

In the next section, I will be discussing how to consciously manifest for the future, but for now, let's move on to clarity in body. The wonderful thing about shifting toward a clear mind is that very same clarity is automatically expressed in the physical body on an energetic level. The body, in other words, is a reflection of the mind;

it's an expression of it. The clearer you become in mind, the higher the thoughts you will choose regarding the mind. As you do so, you will become aware that you can also choose higher thoughts for the body, such as, "I am healthy and whole," "I am comfortable in my own skin," "I am peaceful and that peace is reflected in the physical," and "I am healthier and stronger with each passing day." This way of thinking, whether it is for mind or body, is not based in wishful thinking, but in the knowing that it's happening now. It is a clear and conscious choice. It is coming from a greater awareness, one that is not looking at what *was*, but is based in the potential for a new and greater future through the now.

With regard to the spirit, nothing can be added or taken away from it. Your spiritual self or inner being is clarity personified. All you can do is become more in tune with it through intention, contemplation, meditation, and greater awareness. It is the desired result itself; it is ultimately your main objective and goal because when you consciously become aligned with it, you will remember just what is possible in your life. The spirit or soul then thinks along these lines: "I am potential and possibility." "I am wisdom and clarity." "I am one with Source Energy." All of these conscious, higher-reaching thoughts can be thought and spoken a few times throughout the day. They are energy shifting, empowering, and helpful in that they will help you remain focused on your intentions. Now let's look at some tips and an exercise to become clearer in mind, body, and spirit.

Clarity Tips

• Realize what truly matters in your life and let the small things go.

- Recognize the emotional distractions in your life (i.e., worry or doubt) and see them for what they really are. They are attempts to rob you of your clarity.

- Learn from your past, but make the conscious choice not to relive it.

- See the future as pure potential; nothing is set in stone, despite what fear may say.

- The closer your awareness comes to your spiritual self, the greater the clarity you will experience.

- Clarity is always being offered. Now choose to accept it.

- Your intention for any aspect of your life sets the stage for its manifestation. Be consistent in your decision-making.

- Clarity is a state of being, and it's the most natural state of being you can be in.

• Clarity in Mind, Body, and Spirit Exercise •

When you really think about it, all of life is a meditation. Remember that meditation is simply focus. Every day we're focusing on something, and throughout the day we shift our focus several times. My intention with this exercise is to help you focus on realizing greater clarity in all aspects of your being. Let us begin.

1. Find a quiet space and get comfortable. Take a few deep breaths and center your awareness on the here and now.

2. Next, you're going to invite greater clarity by repeating the following intentions:
   - "I invite and welcome greater clarity."
   - "I am clear in mind, body, and spirit."

- "I am clarity."
- "My intention is the clarity of my inner being."
- "Clarity is all there is."

Be mindful as to just how powerful intentions are and their potential to make shifts in your awareness and life.

3. Spend the next four to five minutes thinking and speaking these higher-vibrating intentions, keeping in mind that your thoughts, words, and decisions shape your reality. Remember that you never want to make or force things to happen. Be patient with yourself and the process. Clarity, like all other spiritual gifts, is received when we are ready to accept it.

4. After four or five minutes, take a few more deep breaths and let the moment go. This exercise can be performed once or twice a week. Keep in mind that less is more.

Manifesting Consciously

Manifesting on a conscious level is a practice of choosing a greater future for yourself through higher thoughts, words, and an elevated vibrational frequency. It's a practice of taking conscious action through higher awareness based in greater clarity. In essence, it involves total engagement—mind, body, and spirit. Let's move into goal and vision setting next and how it ties in with consciously manifesting.

An important step toward aligning yourself with the third eye is to create goals. Do you have a vision for your life? Where would you like to see yourself in five or ten years? Do you want to be of service, perhaps serving humanity in a greater way? What would you call forth if you knew that anything was possible? What do you want to become and what actions do you have to take to make it come to fruition? Personally, I love asking questions because it was questions like these that propelled me forward on my spiritual journey. Questions led me to clarity, which, in this case, was found in sixth chakra activation. They were my fuel for the fire, so to speak. In other words, it was uncertainty and a lack of clarity that led me to take the first few steps of my journey.

It would probably be wise to be mindful of a few things regardless of the vision that you have for your life; I feel these tips may help make your process a little smoother, especially when roadblocks or detours are experienced. You see, although you may have a grand vision for your life, it probably pales in comparison to what Source has in store for you. Source operates this way because it sees the infinite potential within you.

The following is a list that will help you remain focused and in a space of allowing as you bravely and rightfully manifest your destiny. To be honest, it's a list I wish someone had given me several years ago when I began manifesting consciously.

When Manifesting Consciously, Remember…

- Be patient. Trust in the universe's timing.
- Remain flexible. Things are probably not going to unfold exactly the way you want them to.
- Delays are not denials. You're going to continue to grow in the process.
- Practice being in a space of allowing. Recognize and let go of resistance.
- Do what you can and then move out of your own way. Allow Source to do the rest.

- Gratitude is the attitude to maintain.

- Don't compare yourself to someone else's journey. It only leads to frustration.

- Continuous self-development is important.

- Maintain your enthusiasm and passion. Especially during the times where it seems like nothing is happening, be confident that it is.

- Energy goes where your attention goes. Focus on the vision, not the circumstances.

Find Your Purpose

I felt it was of great value to mention how important it is to find your life purpose and to honor it by heeding the soul's call. By actively seeking to discover your passion and strengths, you will save yourself a lot of time, struggle, and frustration. Finding your life's purpose needs a starting point, some self-inquiry. And it begins by asking the right questions. With that being said, here are some questions you can ask yourself to help you zero in on your passions and strengths. Feel free to expand on these questions.

1. How do I like/love to express myself?

2. Am I drawn to writing?

3. Do I enjoy speaking to individuals or large groups? Or both?

4. What psychic abilities have I experienced?

5. Which psychic abilities seem to express themselves the easiest for me?

6. Have I experienced a particular psychic ability (or a group of abilities) more than others?

7. Do I find that some psychic gifts require little effort while others require more work?

8. What is my ideal vision for my life?

9. What would give me the greatest fulfillment?

10. How do I go about realizing this dream?

Whatever purpose you're called to answer, I am certain that it will be an experience of mind, body, and spirit. It's your soul that inspires and seeks expression. It's your mind that creates, focuses, and moves energy. Finally, it's your body that experiences that inspiration and creation with all of your senses.

Develop Your Strengths

Once you've found your passion and recognized your strengths, it's time to develop them in a variety of ways. To begin with, this entails effort and action on your part. It's a holistic approach that includes intuitively listening to your higher wisdom, creating a plan for execution, and following through by doing. I've come up with a list that can help you stir up your creativity, guide you to action, and help you develop your psychic abilities.

- Keep a pad of paper and pen nearby at all times to jot down inspiration whenever it strikes.
- Write down your dreams and aspirations.
- Become a voracious reader.
- See everyone as a teacher and a messenger. (Become an active listener!)
- Look for the signs.
- Take self-development courses.

- Attend lectures.
- Network in spiritual circles.
- Attend spiritual expos.
- Open your mind to possibility.
- Find a teacher that can accelerate your progress.
- Explore different aspects of spirituality.
- Work on centering yourself through practices such as meditation.
- Trust the process.
- Ask questions.
- Do what you love.
- Travel when you can.
- Challenge yourself and move out of your comfort zone.
- Spend time in nature.
- Surround yourself with other creative people.

Moving Past Your Comfort Zone

The thing about operating from the sixth chakra is that once it's activated, you feel more and you sense more. I have heard and read about how some empaths see it as a blessing and a curse, but it doesn't have to be the latter. It doesn't have to be energetically draining, in other words. The practice of being comfortable amidst your own negative emotions or those of others is one of mastery.

There are a few things to keep in mind when experiencing any negative emotion that contrasts to your higher dimensions of consciousness. Resistance is futile; just accept the fact that the ego is what it is and any reaction to it will only perpetuate any remaining grip it may have on your consciousness. Allow negative emotions to pass and remember the temporary nature of them, their coming and going. The presence, the soul within you, is more than capable of transforming and dissolving any negative emotion, regardless of how dark its appearance may be through quiet observation.

Don't get me wrong, I quite enjoy my solitude, but we live in a world of contrast. Everyone is experiencing varying levels of awareness, and therefore varying degrees of emotion and consciousness. And we have to interact with others (unless you choose to live alone high on a mountaintop somewhere). Therefore, bless the differences. See the gift in contrast. Allow others to be who they are through your own self-acceptance. It's an empowering practice because through acceptance, there is no room for reaction, only peace and harmony.

Operating from an activated sixth chakra is the end of personal suffering in that you no longer identify with the ego. It is freedom from fear. But that doesn't mean the contrast stops, and understanding this will further assist you in your own spiritual development. So get comfortable, relax, and allow the unfolding of consciousness within you.

Unlimited Potential

Look at the world around you. Step outside and look up at the starry sky. All that you see is the expression of consciousness. But it doesn't stop there, because all that you don't see—the space, the nothingness—is consciousness also. It's everywhere, in everything, and it is expressing itself as you. In other words, the same energy that gives birth to planets, stars, solar systems, and the entire universe and beyond is within you, and by nature, it's creative.

This unseen, unheard, unfelt, unknowing, unlimited creative force can be recognized, heard, felt, and known through direct experience. Does this sound too good to be true? Well, it's not. It's simply the experience that comes with third eye activation and operating through higher dimensions of consciousness. And once this experience has taken place, which is the remembrance of or rejoining of The All That Is, you will be reminded of just what is possible: anything. The potential that comes with this alignment is limitless, in other words.

The closer you are to being your authentic self, the more emotional barriers are dropped. The more barriers that are dropped, the greater your allowing is. The greater your allowing is, the more you untie Source's hands to deliver what you desire. An unlimited mindset further brings you into greater alignment with your spiritual self.

How to Achieve an Unlimited Mindset

1. Know that all things are possible when you are in alignment with Source Energy, which is an awareness of oneness supported by gratitude and a spirit of allowing or nonresistance.

2. The past does not have to define your present (nor your future, for that matter).

3. Know that you are loved unconditionally, and you are deserving and capable of extending that same love.

4. Miracles are the status quo.

5. Thoughts, words, deeds, and your vibrational frequency are all creative.

6. Let go of the idea that bigger dreams are somehow harder to manifest.

7. What you think is possible is what the universe thinks is possible for you.

8. There are no limits to consciousness.

9. The universe wants to deliver all that you desire. Are you in agreement?

10. There is nothing that you cannot be, do, or have. (Notice the order: being, doing, having.)

chapter five

AWARENESS AND DEVELOPMENT

By now you're probably getting a glimpse of the enormous power and potential that is available through chakra activation. And through greater spiritual awareness, you're elevating your consciousness and arriving at a vantage point that enables you to see yourself and life with greater clarity. With greater understanding comes even deeper, bigger questions, like: Is there truly a purpose in adversity? Can the world really wake up to higher dimensions of consciousness? What would an awakened world look like?

In looking at adversity, whether it be a lack of abundance or a health crisis, a successful way I personally approached these circumstances was to focus on the inner problem solver, the Source within, rather than the effect or the circumstance. When I was faced with cancer fifteen years ago, I experienced an array of emotions; I went from being shocked to frustrated and angry to being confused. These emotions then led me to start asking questions like "Why did this happen?" and "What's the purpose in all this?" Clarity is always preceded by confusion, it seems. It was the asking of questions that started the momentum to receive answers. And personally, I wanted to know how to make my life work. I wasn't going to be satisfied with anything less. Looking back at adversity through the eye of clarity, understanding tells me that it can be one of two things: it can keep you stuck, further perpetuating what is, or it can be a catalyst to transformation and an inner awakening. In other words, there is great potential and possibility in adversity; there are many hidden blessings and lessons that we usually only become aware of once we've come out on the other side.

From a third-dimensional perspective, it may appear at times that the world is going to hell in a handbasket. Just turn on the news and you will likely see a segment on war or conflict, demonstrations of separateness and cries for help. But from an elevated point of view, one realizes that just as adversity and drama are needed to awaken an individual, so too must it be in the collective. After all, the collective is only a reflection of individual consciousness. All of life is a mirror because it's all in your mind. In order to experience a new world—one based in oneness, in higher consciousness—you're going to have to turn your attention from outward to inward and envision the world you desire to experience. It takes a redirection of focus from the effect, or what is, to the cause and what could be. It's going to take many more awakened souls on this planet to assist in elevating the collective's vibrational frequency, but rest assured, it's already happening. One person operating from an activated sixth chakra has the power to positively affect millions through their vibrational frequency because the energy is continuously expanding.

An awakened world will literally be the experience of heaven on earth. Individual consciousness will know and experience oneness with the collective. People will work together, not against each other. Amazing and astonishing scientific discoveries will be made possible because there will be free access to higher dimensions of consciousness. The planet will be recognized as a living entity and be respected as such, allowing for planetary healing. And although there will always be challenges, those challenges will be faced with greater faith and trust, the forces that make all things possible.

Response versus Reaction

A powerful and energy-shifting way to bring you closer to chakra activation is the practice of responding rather than reacting. The former is a conscious choice that is based in expanded awareness and the latter is based in third-dimensional consciousness, which is our human conditioning. Let's start by discussing what reaction is and how it keeps one anchored to third-dimensional consciousness initially. But first, let me be clear—reaction is necessary as a form of communication until it's no longer serving you. Reaction is a way of projecting one's discontentment about something or someone. But it also serves a purpose by layering more and more emotion over you, thereby eventually bringing about emotional heaviness, which can then become a catalyst for an inner shift. You see, there's a common misconception that "letting it all out" somehow releases you of that emotion, whether it be anger or rage, but the truth is, you're only energizing it further by vocalizing it. Remember, words have power, even more so than when they are thought alone. This is why it's always wise to cool off. Deal with the reactions internally on a conscious level rather than speaking in anger, for example, because most of the time, we say things we didn't really mean and once said, it's impossible to take back. Reactions are also viral in nature; they tend to provoke further reactions in others.

A more conscious, empowering approach is to respond, whether it is a circumstance or a person. Responding clears the emotion out of the way and allows higher dimensions of consciousness to come into play. It comes from a place of knowing and trusting that a solution has already been given; it just has to be allowed to present itself. Responding takes spiritual maturity; you must see the bigger picture and realize the temporariness in the situation. Those who practice being responsive also practice forgiveness. They understand the strength in forgiveness, and they release power in it by choosing to let things go rather than perpetuating them. Because conscious responders are mindful of their emotions and how those emotions affect their vibrational frequency, they see the futility in reacting and the power in responding.

Nonattachment

Nothing gives you greater emotional control and control over the ego than the practice of nonattachment. That includes being unattached to outcomes. The moment you let go of trying to control, you gain control—funny, isn't it? Another word to describe nonattachment would be freedom. Nonattachment is freedom in the sense that your energy now flows freely, as it's supposed to, rather than being focused and stuck on a particular situation or end result.

You may have noticed that we're not conditioned to be nonattached. People are rather attached to outcomes and the emotions linked to them. It would be accurate to say, then, what you're attached to has in fact attached itself to you. In other words, like attracts like. What you become in any particular moment is what you attract. Being fearful attracts more fear. Being happy attracts more happy feelings. This is the attractive power you have—you become what you focus upon.

The art of practicing nonattachment frees you of unnecessary emotional burdens. Another benefit is that you're no longer chasing things. Instead, you allow things to flow easily to you. This conscious practice engages sixth chakra consciousness, and its foundation is built upon faith and trust. Operating through inner knowing, trusting the process becomes a way of life and opens the door to a trustworthy future, not one based on uncertainty and doubt. I have always found it quite remarkable, miraculous even, how something so seemingly innocuous, the practice of letting go, can be so empowering and transformative. With that being said, I'm now going to offer you a simple exercise that you can employ whenever you're feeling attached to a certain outcome or negative emotion.

• Nonattachment Exercise •

1. The first step is to recognize when you're feeling attachment. It always shows up as emotion and is usually fear of some loss or the feeling of losing control over a situation.

2. Once you've realized you are experiencing attachment, ask yourself this question: "How is it helping me to worry by wanting a certain result or outcome so badly?" Keep in mind that attachment should be seen as a sign that you are energetically out of alignment and need to get back into a state of flow and nonresistance. You see, whenever you're

in a state of resistance, you're at odds with your inner being and whatever circumstance you're facing.

3. Realize that you have a choice—you can choose differently. When the vibration of attachment appears, observe the emotion of it rather than *becoming* that particular emotion. This is, in essence, the art of letting go and allowing. It's the art of replacing fear with a confidence in your inner being. When you're in a state of allowing and have confidence in the process, you are inviting potential and possibility in.

Mystical Experiences

Altered states of consciousness through meditation can lead to profound spiritual experiences and knowledge that one could not have known otherwise. These are usually communication events between an individual and their soul or highest self. A profound occurrence—usually brief, spontaneous, and intermittent—delivers a powerful and energy-shifting message. The experience could come in a variety of ways; here are a few examples: an audible voice, a near-death experience, a vision, or a combination of vision and voice. Regardless of how these spiritual events come to manifest, they most certainly accomplish their intended goal, which is to open the door to greater understanding and perception.

Incredibly transforming, mystical experiences offer glimpses into the infinite and cement what the individual already believes or knows deep within: there are no limits to consciousness. Being incredibly efficient, the universe will opt to use the fewest number of words to get the message across. And one thing I know for sure is this: there will be no denying what one has experienced because the event is *that* profound. Mystical experiences are also healing in some way, whether it be emotional or physical.

Because of their connection to Source, these powerful and spiritual brushes with the infinite are life changing and often assist in directing one's spiritual journey.

As difficult as it is to fully describe such an experience, the words that come to mind are feelings of oneness, deep awareness, insight, joy, release, and transcendence. Miracle is another word I would use to describe these higher-dimensional experiences. In other words, mystical experiences defy time and space, operating beyond the physical laws known to human beings.

The following are some ways you can open yourself up to the possibility of a mystical experience. It's important to note that these experiences cannot be forced; they are in fact spontaneous in nature.

Opening Yourself Up to the Possibility of a Mystical Experience

1. Make meditation a part of your daily life, and do so without any expectation whatsoever.

2. Practice maintaining a higher-vibrational frequency by challenging negative thinking and living more presently.

3. Come from a space that knows all things are possible.

4. Realize that you are a part of a conscious universe.

5. Increase your awareness by being focused wherever you are.

6. Live with gratitude.

7. Realize that miracles happen every day.

8. Become more aware, within and without. In other words, open your eyes to your inner and outer world and seek to see more and feel more.

Spiritual Reality

We are at the cusp of an emerging, spiritual-reality-based consciousness where the belief in separation will be left behind, allowing what has always been present to shine through the individual and collective consciousness. This oneness-based reality will be the result of an activated sixth chakra where single vision becomes the dominant perception. Through clear inner vision, one sees oneself beyond male or female, color or creed, or any other form of identification. One simply sees and directly experiences Source Energy expressing itself in an infinite number of ways.

This new reality is the return to the safety and certainty of inner stillness. Being the channel for peace, the individual will see the futility in self-created dramas and inner conflict and will consciously leave it behind, allowing for new, life-giving experiences. Creativity will become one of the main focuses of life, the free expression of the soul without any form of limitation. As more people come into their authentic selves, humanity as a whole will come closer to reaching a critical mass—a tipping point, if you will—where the vibrational frequency of the awakened few will be powerful enough to cause spontaneous awakenings in the many.

This spiritual chain reaction, so to speak, is already underway. We are witnessing the awakening of humanity. Individual awakening can no longer be limited to the few; it is a collective necessity if this planet is going to heal and move toward peace and unity. For many, the ego has grown to be quite dark by nature, and there is no way to change it; one can only move past it. Fear is fear, plain and simple. You can try to paint it another color, but its essence will always remain the same.

The Power of Decision and Focus

Two incredibly life-changing spiritual faculties, the harnessing of the energy-shifting power of decision and focus, can make the difference between defeat and victory in the fulfillment of desire. The power of decision is based in your will, and your will is always fueled by desire. And what is desire but the universe wanting to express itself through you, as you? Therefore, know and understand this: What you desire and will for your life is what Source Energy desires and wills for your life. You are the director and the universe is the producer. You literally call forth experience through desire and the power of decision. As a side note, be mindful that it's not desire that truly creates suffering, but the attachment to outcomes. Desire is the spark, the initial catalyst that ignites the universal engine of manifestation.

When I was searching for an empowering way to live, I refused to let the adversities laid before me stop me. I wasn't going to allow my circumstances or negative emotions like fear, doubt, or uncertainty stop me from finding answers. Decision is what shapes your destiny. Decision is a life-moving energy when made by a willing and earnest spirit.

Fueled by decision, focus is the accompanying force that allows you to hone your vision. The thing about focus is that it clears your mind, allowing a vision to become clear in your mind's eye. Clear focus directs universal energy and allows it to flow toward the intended goal. And the clearer the focus, the more straightforward the path will be. Focus doesn't vacillate, but allows for needed change. It brings your awareness to a possible future; initially engaging hope, it quickly moves on to an inner state of knowing through developed faith and trust.

I felt it was quite important to touch upon these two spiritual faculties in particular because they open doors to possibility, allow for greater clarity, and have a way of moving universal energy. They are transformative in nature, stirring the soul to take action and creating a way when there doesn't seem to be one. In other words, decision and focus are the keys to potential and what could be—what is already waiting for you—in the unseen quantum field of consciousness.

Truth and Illusion

Many people today are seeking truth, and they're searching for something bigger than themselves. So let's take a deeper look at truth and the matter of illusion. The desire to know and remember is the soul's yearning to know itself experientially while with the body here on Earth. The thing about truth is that it really can't be given to you; it's already within you. It is a part of your soul as inner stillness. A teacher can point you inward, remind you of some truths, and even inspire you, but truth is what is within you and it's what is found the moment your sixth chakra is activated. A profound and ineffable mystical experience, your spiritual awakening will be your rebirth into the field of limitless possibility.

Everyone is here on their own path to remember who they are because, through human conditioning or the ego, they've forgotten. But the good news is that just because you've forgotten something doesn't mean that it's lost forever. You cannot completely lose something that is always a part of you.

On to the topic of illusion and the source of it: the false self known as the ego. In order to shed light on what illusion is, let's look at reality first. The authentic self is found in stillness, inner stillness. It's pure and unconditional love. It's unchanging, eternal, and beyond shape or form. It is always anchored in the now. The authentic self is transcendent in every way. It is beyond all emotion. Illusion, on the other hand, is what constantly changes. It comes in many forms: emotions, the past, the future … In other words, it's the ego in a nutshell. A dreaming state, illusions are seductive and attempt to replace and blanket the reality of stillness within you. Completely transient in nature, the only certainty offered through illusion is doubt. No one can dictate to you what illusion or truth is; it's your free will to decide. In other words, don't believe everything you read or hear, but if what's being offered resonates with you, if it raises your vibrational frequency, then you may choose to accept it. I've compiled a list of some spiritual truths, reminders that have high vibrational energy to them. These spiritual truths will speak to many of you regardless of where you are on your spiritual path.

Spiritual Truths to Remember

- We are always connected to Source Energy. Separation is an illusion.
- The ego is not who you are, but an accumulation of past experiences and perspectives that are also a potential catalyst to chakra activation.
- You are an eternal spiritual being having a temporary human experience.
- We always receive what we project or extend because all is one.
- There are no limits to consciousness, and no limits are put upon you except those that are self-imposed.

- All matter is spiritual energy in form.

- Faith and trust make all things possible.

- The past and future are mental constructs; the now is all there really is.

- Peace, happiness, and joy are all inside jobs.

- You are unconditional love, an extension of Source Energy.

- Everything is a miracle, and this is fully recognized through higher dimensions of awareness.

- Love is the only reality and the greatest force in the universe.

chapter six

INSPIRATION, GUIDANCE, AND CREATIVITY

Have you ever tried giving really good advice to a friend who was just not listening, not tuning in to what you were saying? You could say that they weren't getting the message because they were on a different frequency, with a different vibe than the one you were coming from. And because of that, they weren't able to hear the message or see the value in it. I'm willing to go out on a limb and say we've all tried to be good friends by offering counsel at one time or another. As spiritual beings, we sometimes experience insight into our friends' or family's lives and can see what's around the corner, so to speak. But if the receiver is not ready or willing to receive the information, then it goes unheard.

What I've just shared is what our spirit guides would like to get across today, right here and now. They want us to know that they know the path. They are always offering guidance but are not always listened to. And they're saying it's usually for one of two reasons: we're either not aware when we're being guided, or we know we're being guided but choose otherwise because of free will.

I'm a big fan of lists as they make things more direct, and they allow for better focus. The following is a list of ten things you can undertake to allow for greater clarity as you become further aware that you're always being guided.

Tips for Receiving Guidance and Making Better Decisions

1. Tune in to guidance more often and actively listen.

2. Become more aware of the world around you. Look for signs.

3. Invite meditation to become a part of your day, even for a few minutes.

4. Pay attention to what your body requires nutritionally.

5. Universal cues abound. Simply look for them.

6. Connect with the outdoors.

7. Visualize your desires and create the feelings of their fulfillment.

8. Let go of the past so that a new future can be called forth.

9. Ask questions because they tend to lead to answers.

10. Remember that you are never without spiritual guidance.

Asking Questions

I really like to ask questions because it's a habit that I found invaluable during the beginning of my spiritual path. What I didn't know at the time was that by asking questions, I was setting the stage to receive answers. The answers didn't arrive instantly, but they did arrive—on their own terms and with perfect timing.

The questions I asked signaled to the universe that I desired understanding. I simply wanted to know. I wanted to understand how life worked, why things happen the way they do, and what the purpose in all of this was. And I wasn't going to stop asking questions until I received the clarity and knowledge I was thirsting for. With that being said, are there any questions about your life (or about life in general) that you want answered?

Asking questions—specifically deep, meaningful questions—has a way of shaping your destiny. By questioning what is, you can find out what could be. There is great energy behind the seeking of answers and solutions. Questions have a way of leading you to the right book, the right person, or the right place where the answer is waiting for you. By asking questions, you place yourself in a space of flexibility, an open-mindedness that perhaps there's more than the eye can see.

The other thing to keep in mind is to ask the right kind of questions. Ask the most valuable questions: the ones that seek clarity, understanding, and wisdom. These types of questions draw the attention of the universe because they come from deep desire. Sincerity, it seems, goes a very long way.

Take a few moments and think of some questions you'd like answered. Ask yourself these questions. Then get ready, because the answers are already in queue; they are just waiting to be offered to you.

Inspired and Guided toward Creativity

All of us have a creative side, which is sourced from our inner being. The soul is inspiration itself, and it's always trying to get that inspiration to the forefront of your awareness. The key to becoming more aware of inspired thought is to really pay attention to the cues as they come in the form of feelings, spiritual nudges, visions, or even external experiences, such as seeing someone doing something that you're aspiring to do.

Now, the soul will use a variety of ways to get the particular message across. You have an inner guidance system that will actually give you a metaphorical green or red light on the matter at hand. I've created a list of ways to discern when you're being inspired and guided toward creativity, also well as two tips on when something is perhaps not for you and you should not proceed further.

If You're Being Inspired and Guided to Proceed…

- The idea feels uplifting.
- You can't help but feel a jolt of energy. When a great idea is recognized it's usually met with excitement, and it has a way of raising your energy field.
- When you contemplate the idea, there is no resistance within you.
- It is in alignment with your desires.
- Looking at the end result—the fulfillment of your desire— you take a moment and ask yourself, "Is this a step toward its fulfillment?" If the answer is "Yes," you're on your way toward its manifestation.
- You feel passion and enthusiasm while you're creating.
- You're feeling great love for what you're doing because love is being expressed.
- For the most part, it feels effortless.
- There might be some detours along the way, but the thing you're doing comes easily to you; you have found your purpose.

- You find signs and synchronicities along the way. It may be a repeating message in a fortune cookie, or you might see a bumper sticker that says something like, "You're on the right track." These are just some of the ways the universe could let you know you're on the right path.

- Inspiration is flowing on an ongoing basis. This is a telltale sign you're being guided and that you're in tune with your life's purpose.

- It feels like a whole approach, one where you create on all levels. In other words, it feels authentic, a mind-body-spirit experience. This is probably the most important and obvious way to tell that you're being inspired and guided toward creativity.

When Not to Proceed

- Anything that is not in alignment with your highest good will result in the soul railing against it. You may feel a knot in the pit of your stomach or have a negative feeling about proceeding forward. Honor these feelings.

- You feel no enthusiasm or passion about moving forward with the idea.

Feel Your Way

Your conscious mind, your very own awareness that you operate from daily, is being called by the soul. Like a beacon of light dimmed by the clouds of thinking, it's partially covered but never extinguished. Navigating your awareness back to the Source within requires an inner journey, one toward the safety and certainty of inner stillness. The closer one is to Source, the more relaxed, confident, and in a state of allowing they're in. One way to navigate your way back to the self is to go by feel, using your emotional guidance system. As you come into closer conscious proximity to your highest self, you will experience greater joy, clarity, and peace. As you navigate past the ego's thought system, you will find that the mind quiets to a point where the inner dialogue is transcended and all that is left is pure awareness.

In this state of pure awareness, all ego constructs fade away because the vibration is beyond what the ego can handle. As you tune out the ego, you automatically tune in to infinite intelligence. Again, one must fall, so to speak, for the other to rise. Initially, this experience in pure awareness lasts momentarily, but it can last longer and longer through meditation and mindfulness practices. Being in this space of awareness is what opens the door to miracles and mystical experiences, including a spontaneous third eye opening. I also refer to this awareness as the field of unlimited potential and possibility.

Making the conscious return back to this quantum field, which I will discuss later on, is your return back home while still being here on Earth. It's an experience in unconditional love and support. An endless fountain of energy, this field is restorative and balancing by nature, allowing for energetic healing. One enters this quantum world leaving self-imposed limitations behind as psychic abilities are remembered, bringing to your awareness just who and what you really are. Experiences in channeling, automatic writing, and clairvoyance (just to name a few abilities) become the new norm as this field of awareness is allowed to be expressed through you.

Be aware that what you are seeking is most certainly seeking you. The soul has the desire to experience itself while with the physical body. It desires this because it's one thing to know what it's capable of, but it is another to actually manifest it or experience it through the physical body. Pay attention to the emotional signs using your gauge of feeling. Lower-vibrating energies push you farther from the authentic self while uplifting feelings pull you inward—closer to who you are, in essence.

Let's take a moment and look at ten tips to enhance your ability to feel your way back to the source of your inspiration and creativity, which is your inner being.

Ten Ways to Return to Your Inner Being

1. The direct experience of the soul is a feeling, and that feeling is unconditional love, which is free from any fear.

2. Forgive others. Doing this (even within your own mind) has a way of raising your vibrational frequency, thereby bringing you closer to your spiritual self.

3. Don't be afraid of your feelings. Embrace them. Moving toward negative emotion and seeing that emotion through the eyes of nonreaction is powerful and transformative.

4. Be gentler with yourself and others. In other words, lighten up.

5. Know that your spiritual self is as close as your own breath.

6. When you feel inspiration, follow that feeling right back to its source, your soul.

7. Practice going inward. There's a whole other world there waiting to be remembered and experienced.

8. Recognize the soul's attributes, like peace, joy, and a sense of well-being. When you experience these feelings, be mindful that these are reflections of your inner being.

9. Stir up passion and enthusiasm within yourself to grow closer to your spiritual self.

10. Practice going with the flow; the soul is nonresistant in essence.

Building Momentum

Let's say you've been inspired, got creative, and felt that initial guidance to take action. The next step is to build on that initial idea and find ways to deal with the things that may try to stop you along the way, things like fear (the fear of failure in particular), doubt, and uncertainty. These adversaries will no doubt rear their ugly little heads whenever you decide to venture into a new direction or into the unknown.

You must remain motivated while building momentum to manifest your inspired thought. These tips will help keep you moving forward so you can see your goal realized.

Eight Ways to Stay Motivated

1. **Ask yourself this question: "Where will I be in one year if I don't take daily, consistent action toward my goal?"** This is an important question to ask, one that comes with an obvious answer. You see, remaining motivated requires a daily, concerted effort. Even taking consistent action for one hour a day can provide you with tremendous results. Not only that, it will give you the fulfillment and satisfaction of knowing you're moving closer to your dreams.

2. **Say no to fear.** Fear can become your greatest obstacle if you allow it to. Because of that, you have to be aware of it and face it. You face it by seeing it as a conditioned response, an automatic negative thought. Remember, it's just a thought; you have the power to energize it with reaction or neutralize it by witnessing it and then letting it go. As for the fear of failure, remember that it's all a process. You will learn what works and what doesn't along the way. If something does not work out as planned or "fails," learn from it, but

don't let it stay with you. Failure is usually part of the process. You have to be willing to experience failure on your path to greatness.

3. **Have fun along the way.** This is important because taking the time to enjoy yourself while working toward making a dream come true can actually lead you to even more inspiration! Doing what you love, whether that is going for a walk or seeing a movie, puts you in a relaxed state and makes you more open to receiving guidance and wisdom. So make sure to schedule time for yourself to just do what makes you happy on a daily basis.

4. **Surround yourself with like-minded people who are supportive.** No one wants to be around a pessimist, especially when you're in the process of realizing a goal. Finding even one or two people who are as enthusiastic and passionate as you can make all the difference. You can inspire one another, ideas can be bounced off each other, and together you can find solutions.

5. **Write out some deadlines on a calendar.** I've used this approach more than a few times and have always found it beneficial. Giving yourself a week or a month to achieve something is action inducing. If it's clearly written with a bright marker, you're going to look at it daily, and that will give you the added incentive to get moving.

6. **Listen to inspiring people.** A few times a week, set aside time to listen to your favorite inspirational speaker, author, or anyone who inspires you. And when you do, remember to give those moments all of your attention, because you never know what you might hear. At any given moment, guidance could be speaking to you.

7. **Little steps will multiply.** Momentum is built like this: little actions are repeated day after day until so much motion has been built behind them that a figurative tsunami of energy is created, and one day, that energy propels you forward. In other words, there is no such thing as a small action; each step is vital to creating the desired momentum.

8. **Stay positive ... or not.** Yes, it's good to be positive and maintain that energy most of the time, but don't be hard on yourself when you have a bad day. Remember that this is a world of contrast, and negative emotion is a part of it. Allow yourself to feel negative feelings but don't remain there; remember that an elevated feeling is only a conscious thought away.

Centered and Grounded

As important as it is to feel inspiration and creativity and to remember that you're a spiritual being, it's just as important to be able to center and ground yourself. A balance is needed, as too much of anything is not ideal. Let's look at ways to merge your spiritual and human aspects through a mindful approach.

As you integrate being a spiritual being with being human, there are many things you can apply and remember to help you maintain balance while building a solid spiritual foundation. Through centeredness, your awareness is planted in the now. Your energy is focused on creating your life consciously, leaving limiting beliefs behind while fear loses its power in the present moment. Fear needs your belief in the future to perpetuate itself, and by realizing this one instant—the now—you revoke its power and reclaim yours. Through the practice of being grounded, you can fully experience the safety and protection of spirit. You can experience greater stability and ease as a human being. Being grounded also makes you more than capable of responding to any given situation rather than reacting.

The important thing to remember is that this is a process, an unfolding of consciousness that requires patience, self-nurturing, and flexibility. As you embark on an exponentially more conscious and empowering way of living, there are a few things to be mindful of—because keep in mind, enlightenment is only the beginning. For example, the temptations and old habits sponsored by the ego will still try to pull you back. Through higher awareness, you will be able to recognize these illusions for what they are: the past trying to haunt you. By operating through higher dimensions of consciousness, you'll become increasingly aware of any form of negativity, allowing you to dissolve it as it arises. Through inner stillness, you'll also be able to experience a vast spectrum of emotions while knowing and remembering where center is.

Taking the best of both worlds—the experience of being human and the adversity that comes with that from time to time—along with the clarity, strength, wisdom, and understanding that springs forth from an activated chakra makes for a fully integrated and grounded person. Compassion, then, comes from knowing that every soul is on a sacred path back to oneness. Every soul is dealing with their own adversities and challenges as best they know how. This awareness is also a tremendous gift in contrast; although you may have reached the intended goal of expanded awareness, there are still others waiting to be reminded of who they really are. Human-spirit integration, then, is having one foot firmly on the ground; it's the humanity in you while you continue to allow the continuous expansion of your consciousness as you merge with Source Energy.

The following is an exercise in centering and grounding. It only takes two or three minutes to do but can really help you get through the day whenever you're feeling energetically out of alignment.

• Centering and Grounding Exercise •

1. Find a quiet space. Take three or four deep breaths while relaxing your shoulders. On the last deep breath, bring your awareness to the now.

2. Affirm the following:

   • "I am centered in the present."

   • "Life is right here, right now."

   • "I am a spiritual being having a human experience."

   • "Being human does not for one moment diminish my spirituality."

3. Repeat these affirmations for one minute.

4. Take a deep breath and let the moment go.

You can also center and ground yourself by taking a walk in nature, spending fifteen minutes walking barefoot on grass, or taking one of your palms and pressing it against a tree for a few minutes. Any time you reconnect with nature and the stillness of it, you move closer to your inner being, elevating yourself energetically. This, in turn, is the spiritual acknowledgment that balances being human.

chapter seven

CLARITY AND WISDOM

Old, limiting habits can be broken and more empowering ones can most certainly be embraced as you get into the forward flow of consciousness and allow the unfolding of it within you. When it comes to the power of consciousness, the amount of time that has passed, your age, background, or circumstances are inconsequential to it. Time has no impact on the eternal; neither does what you've been through or where you've been. Those things don't matter to Source Energy. No, what Source has interest in is who you're being in any given moment. Source wants us to go inward and return to the safety of our inner being.

This is why meditation is such a large part of spiritual life. In fact, meditation becomes a way of life at the level of mastery. Everything becomes a meditation through an activated sixth chakra. But you don't have to wait until your sixth chakra is activated to bring meditation into your daily life. In a nutshell, meditation is focused awareness. The more you practice it, the more profound the experience and the easier it becomes to enter that transcendent space of awareness. What's also important in this particular case is to remove any idea that getting to such a level of awareness is difficult or impossible because the truth is, it's the most natural thing you could ever do.

Ask yourself, "How difficult could it be to live through my authentic self?" Then ask yourself, "How hard is it living through the ego with all its negative emotions and limitations?" Your highest self is a master meditator; it's the silent inner being, unmoved and unshakeable. This is where you want to place your focused awareness. And the more you do this, the greater the peace, harmony, and relaxation you'll experience, allowing spiritual gems of wisdom to spontaneously come to the surface of your mind. Intuition is much easier to perceive (as are other psychic abilities) in this wakeful, relaxed state. Clarity replaces confusion and things just begin to make more spiritual sense. And universal intelligence, your nonlocal self, takes the wheel, guiding and supporting you.

The benefits of being mindful—present and wakeful—are almost too many to count, but it's not out of the ordinary to experience more energy, heightened awareness, improved blood pressure, an improved ability to handle stress, and greater clarity, just to name a few. Here are some things to be mindful of as you start to bring meditation into your daily life.

Meditation Points to Remember

- "Meditation is my natural state of being. In fact, inner stillness is a reflection of my inner being."

- "Peace is an extension of my inner being because peace is what I am."

- "I am expressing my authentic self through the awareness of it."

- "My psychic abilities are more easily expressed through a still mind."

- "A quiet mind is a reflection of the universal mind, which is the field of limitless potential and miracles."

- "Just being aware of the present moment is a meditation in and of itself."

- "When I am in the space of inner stillness, my soul is allowed to express joy, love, and happiness without anything external having to change first."

- "Nothing is lost in meditation, but my whole self is found."

- "Meditation opens the door to soul communication, and stillness is the language of the soul."

- "What I am seeking is found through meditation. It's the doorway to higher dimensions of consciousness and new realities."

Maintaining Clear Vision

Masters of meditation approach life by being mindful and remembering who and what they are on a moment-by-moment basis. They are centered and remember their oneness. Over time, the practice of engaging the conscious mind throughout the day becomes an automatic and effortless practice. It's the conscious choosing of reality over illusion, unconditional love over fear. It's knowing who you are relative to Source Energy and understanding what you're not. You may experience fear, but you are not fear. You may experience doubt, but you are not doubt. You may experience anger, but you are not anger. You may experience guilt, but you are not guilt. No degree of darkness can ever change what is eternally unchangeable.

Because we are all extensions of Source Energy, we are equipped with the same attributes and the same characteristics. Being made of the "same stuff," the same consciousness, we share the same creative power as Source. If you remove a drop of water from the ocean, it still remains the same, it has the same atomic makeup, it is just not as powerful as it was when it was one with the ocean. If you put that drop of water back into the ocean, it has all the power of that ocean because it has immersed itself; it has become one with it.

Source gives freely of itself, without limits or conditions. But—and this is a big but—if we close ourselves off from this universal force through the idea of separation, then we contract the energy and stop the flow of power. This energy blockage is what leads to uneasiness and confusion. This is why there's such tremendous power in allowing and spiritual alignment; they open the tap to the flow of universal energy and the clear vision that comes with it.

It doesn't get clearer than this: You're here to be the full expression of Source Energy. And that includes expressing all the abilities that are innately yours. If you can remember this, your life's purpose will not only be made clear, but you will maintain that vision and clarity all the days of your life. It really all comes down to the acceptance of your oneness and all that comes with it.

Let It Spill into Action

As you move past the layers of human conditioning, you will begin to experience greater levels of personal freedom and, with that, greater confidence in yourself. Allow that confidence to translate into action. Allow the expression of your inner being to flow into the outside world. Everything is a reflection because of the reality of oneness. In order to experience kindness, you have to express it, demonstrate it, and become it. If you wish to experience forgiveness, extend it to others. Search within your mind and allow those who need to be forgiven to come to the forefront of your consciousness. Think or say, "I forgive you and release you. I bless you." Forgiveness is an incredibly powerful form of prayer; it's the realization of oneness. As you bless the person you're forgiving, you can't help but forgive and bless yourself, for we are all one.

You may also feel like you are being guided to begin to journal your spiritual unfolding, or you may be urged to start writing poetry. This is the soul desiring to communicate with you while expressing its unconditional love through wisdom and understanding. Go with it. Allow yourself to be led and trust the process. In other words, let go and let Source.

Through greater inner awareness, you will automatically be gentler with yourself and others. You will understand yourself and in turn, you will come to understand others. Knowing that everyone is dealing with their own adversity, any thoughts of judgment will turn to compassion. This unconditional love in action results in two outcomes: your personal relationships become elevated, becoming a sharing of completeness through your greater understanding, or they are exited simply because you cannot force change upon anyone—it's always an inside job. Remember, you shouldn't have to lower your vibrational frequency to appease another; it always leads to resentment, and you're not doing anything but feeding the other's ego in the process.

With Wisdom Comes Peace

The peace offered through the channel of the sixth chakra is profound and unchanging. It's not based in material wealth or in relationships, but in your inner being. This otherworldly peace is based in wisdom found in higher dimensions of consciousness. This peace is unshaken by the world or its circumstances. It is unyielding to negative emotion and therefore completely sovereign.

Allowing wisdom to flow to your conscious mind through the channel of the sixth chakra is a matter of alignment and awareness. First, know that wisdom is within you, but it needs to be recognized; it requires your awareness. Everyone experiences moments of wisdom, but not everyone is aware when wisdom is revealed. Through awareness, your attention will continue to travel inward toward the source of wisdom, which is your inner being.

Conscious alignment with your inner being is a matter of shifting to your center. There are two ways to operate: you can live on the surface, where your attention is always on the outside world, focusing on what everyone else is doing; or you can live from a deep awareness, from inner presence. The former is through the ego and the latter is through your inner being. One leads to confusion and indecision while the other leads to clarity and decision.

The following laundry list provides various insights that you can be mindful of to allow wisdom to express through you consciously, thereby strengthening your connection with the third eye. Allow wisdom to flow through you and experience the peace that comes with it.

Wisdom Laundry List

- Wisdom is like any other miracle: natural and spontaneous. There are no limits to Source Energy and because of that, you need to let go of any ideas of limitation. Accept the fact that you are an extension of universal intelligence.

- Wisdom is what you are because you are a part of unconditional love and unconditional love is the source for all your spiritual faculties. Understanding that you are not your ego but the unconditional love being cloaked by it should provide you with the understanding that all that you need to be successful is already within you.

- Peace is a reflection of wisdom. Through wisdom, one gains understanding, and from that understanding self-realization occurs. Through that inner knowing, your authentic self and the peace emanating from it are allowed to be freely expressed.

- Awareness is what gives life, so be aware that wisdom is within you. Awareness, your attention, is what creates your reality. It calls things forth. Therefore, focus on the good and on what you have, not on what you lack.

- Wisdom is discernment; it's knowing who and what you are and understanding what you're not. The wise understand themselves and because of that they see the purpose in contrast, knowing the difference between dark, light, and all the shades in between.

- Wisdom is encoded throughout the universe, present everywhere, as is peace. Because Source is unconditional love, gifts like wisdom, peace, clarity, understanding, and joy are reflections of that love.

• Inner peace is freedom, and that results from the wisdom of self-understanding. Being free of the ego's rule results in inner peace. That freedom is an extension of understanding your personal power and how fragile the ego really is.

• Wisdom and peace are available now—there is no need for delay. You can choose to claim your spiritual inheritance today. Willingness and desire are the keys.

• Inner peace is not just the absence of fear, but the ability to transform it when it presents itself. A quieted mind is a reflection of inner peace. Peace doesn't leave when fear roars. Fear has no power except when you give it your belief.

• Wisdom is a moment-by-moment experience. Living in the present through each and every breath is the practice of wakeful presence, and through that presence, your gifts are allowed to express.

• Your inner being knows the difference between fear and unconditional love. Effort is not required to live through your inner being. In fact, it's a continual process of coming into alignment with your highest self, which is the source of wisdom.

• Opening the door to wisdom leads to greater understanding and miracles. Once you make the return to your inner being, there are no boundaries to what you can understand or experience. There are no limitations to consciousness.

Potential and Inner Workings of the Mind

We're going to now take a deeper look at the mind of Source, its potential, its inner workings, and your connection to it. These insights will give you a greater understanding of the universal energy that you're always working with.

- **Your mind is an extension of the universal mind, and because of that, it's always creating.** Being part of the universal mind means that you too are always in a state of creating and calling forth your own personal reality. This insight is empowering because this means that you and you alone have the power to manifest your destiny. You don't have to focus on your circumstances; rather, decide within yourself what you'd like to manifest in your life and then focus on that. Take action from that vantage point.

- **Because you have free will, you can create your life unconsciously or consciously.** You create your life unconsciously by reliving the past. Create your life consciously through your inner being and the present moment. Nothing in this reality is set in stone. Realize and understand that in every moment there is potential and possibility to change the direction of your life. In other words, don't allow the past to dictate what your present or future will be. You can always choose differently.

- **What you continuously focus on can be manifested in your life, desirable or undesirable—the universe doesn't decide for you, you do.** Focused awareness has potential and possibility. Your continued attention to something can call it forth. Understand that if there has been a long-lasting fear nagging at you, the reason is because you haven't faced it yet and seen it for what it is: an illusion. In other words, we continue to relive or reexperience the things that we haven't learned from yet. Perhaps you need a lesson in nonattachment, forgiveness, or becoming fearless. Whatever is persisting needs to be looked at, addressed, and released.

• **The mind requires direction and your conscious participation, which is achieved by being present and aware.** Whenever you experience runaway thinking (also known as undirected thinking), it should serve as a reminder to pull the reins in energetically speaking and to recenter yourself. Everything serves a purpose, even those moments where things may seem to be falling apart. These moments are saying, "Hey, get back into alignment. Center yourself. You're a little off course." The mind requires direction, a vision, so set a course.

• **The mind has the potential to heal on a spiritual and physical level.** Your mind is the doorway to healing. The healing I am mentioning here is the perceived separation between you and Source Energy. This begins with the realization that you are not separate from Source, but an extension of it. Once oneness has been experienced directly, the healing effects of this experience on all levels—mind, body, and spirit—become quite possible.

• **The ego is not your mind.** The ego is a self-created, separate self, although it will try to convince you otherwise. The thinking mind is what you use, but it's not who you are. You are an eternal spiritual being having an ego and a human experience, both of which are temporary. Clarity is the intention here. If you can understand that the thinking mind is simply the contrast to your inner light, you will begin to allow a greater awareness to rise in your conscious mind. It's this awareness, the reflection of your inner being, that can bring quiet to your mind, allowing spiritual faculties like your psychic abilities to express themselves.

- **Understanding the mind's power leads to greater discernment and greater insight.** But even beyond that, understanding the mind is equal to being in a state of knowing. As you clear up your energy field, you'll begin to experience greater moments of insight. And it's through insight that you can see the world around you more clearly. When your soul or spirit guides communicate with you, it will be clear; there will be no second-guessing.

- **The universal mind houses all alternate realities, and thought is the doorway to those realities.** My intention is to make this statement incredibly easy to understand. Life can be seen as a video game. Within a video game is every possible decision or outcome; you can go left or right, up or down, based on your thoughts or decisions. Life is just like that—every possible decision is already created in the quantum field; the field of the unmanifested is waiting to be called forth. A clear understanding of this field will be offered in the next chapter because your fullest potential is found within the quantum field.

- **The universal mind connects everything and everyone, and you are one with it.** This is how psychics are able to receive information beyond the five senses; they know how to tap in to the universal mind. Psychics and mediums are able to bring themselves into a meditative state where they still their thinking mind and allow for energy information to be received. In other words, they raise their vibrational frequency to the level of the universal mind.

- **The mind is the birthplace for experience, including the mystical and miraculous.** Reflect on this: Everything is taking place within your mind. All of your experiences—the highs and the lows—are reflected as emotions, and emotions are experienced within the mind. Mystical events like a sudden flash of insight, for example, are mind events. People experiencing spontaneous healings also experience these within the confines of their own consciousness.

- **What you will with your mind is what the universal mind wills for you.** To clarify, the desires you have in your heart were in fact placed there by Source. And what you desire to experience is what Source desires. You are choosing and Source Energy is supplying.

- **You are only limited by your imagination.** Imagination is an incredible tool; it's how we set a vision for ourselves. But there is an awareness that goes beyond imagination, and it's found within your unmanifested self. It's this unbound awareness that can spontaneously express as unimaginable experiences when you get out of your own way. Relax and allow the spontaneity of your inner being to produce miracles in your life.

chapter eight

UNDERSTANDING AND ENLIGHTENMENT

My intention for this chapter is to demystify the experience of enlightenment. Enlightenment is actually quite simple in its essence; it's our human conditioning and all the beliefs we've picked up along the way that has made everything so complicated. What I'm going to do in this chapter is describe who you are at the deepest level and then paint a picture of what it's like to operate from this awareness so that you can have a greater understanding of just how possible this inner shift is for you during this lifetime.

You are a mind, body, and spirit, a three-part being. The mind is that part of you that creates, the body takes action, and the spirit inspires. This chapter's focus is the spirit, your inner being, because that is who you are at the deepest level; this is your enlightened self. The inner being is the silent witness within you;

it's the awareness looking through your eyes. Being an extension of Source Energy, your inner being has never judged. It is beyond all perception because it is unconditional love. From that unconditional love flows the many attributes of the spirit, such as wisdom, clarity, understanding, strength, knowing, forgiveness, compassion, joy, and your psychic abilities.

The spirit within you communicates through the frequency of inner stillness. And it speaks softly to you with great clarity and wisdom. If you are being guided by higher wisdom, the information being offered will have a high-vibrational frequency to it, one free of any fear. Always connected with infinite intelligence, the spirit within you knows everything there is to know.

What I want you to understand is that within you is already an enlightened being, fully equipped with all the spiritual faculties needed to make for a successful life. Nothing has to be added to you in order for you to become enlightened. And no one can give you what is already yours. A spiritual teacher can point you inward and offer you insights, but the last step is for you to take. In other words, a teacher can walk you to the door, but it is yours to open. You must have the desire and willingness to enter.

It's important to mention that there's nothing special about enlightenment. It's simply a more empowering and conscious way to live. You don't become better than anyone else; you just become a greater version of who you once were. You still put your pants on one leg at a time.

What I want to talk about now is the experience of enlightenment. In the state of enlightenment, you don't lose yourself; you merge your awareness with your inner being, which is one with Source. The mind is quieted because you are in alignment with spirit and its reflection is the peace of inner stillness. You still experience fear, but it no longer dominates your thinking; it loses its power over you. It becomes an awareness of the darkness of the ego and the light of your true consciousness. You experience the power of choice and consciously choose empowering, high-vibrating thoughts that are a result of wisdom and understanding. You observe rather than react to the ego's thought system. In the state of enlightenment, you live in the present moment and are fully aware of its reality. You are still aware of the past and future, but now you realize these are simply mental constructs.

What you will most likely come to realize in an awakened state is that you live more in one breath than you ever did in all the time before your enlightenment. It's that profound of an experience. Every encounter becomes a sacred one. You cannot help but extend unconditional love and compassion to everyone you meet because it is radiating from your inner being freely. Energetically speaking, you feel light as a feather, having shed the layers of human conditioning, but at the same time you honor the gift of being human.

Everyday challenges are approached from the vantage point that a solution is already given. Life just flows more easily and without energy-draining resistance. Your intuition becomes incredibly heightened and clarity makes for easy communication between you and your spirit guides. From this level of awareness, you understand that Source supports, cares, and unconditionally loves you, which provides you with a tremendous amount of gratitude and an appreciation for the gift of life.

Third-, Fourth-, and Fifth-Dimensional Realities

Understanding the stages of spiritual awakening or the expansion of awareness is a must for any spiritual seeker or anyone wanting to develop their psychic abilities. I would have really appreciated this information in the weeks and months following my own shift; it would have given me a greater understanding of what was happening at the time. I want to offer you a clear understanding of these realities or levels of awareness that you are in fact already experiencing in varying degrees.

Third-Dimensional Reality

I've previously discussed third-dimensional reality as ego consciousness or the conditioned mind, so I will just briefly touch upon it here for contrast. Third-dimensional reality or awareness is what we are offered the moment we show up on this planet. It is characterized as individual consciousness, where one feels they are separate from their outside world. Identity is usually tied to occupation, material items, and relationships. Keep in mind that there's nothing wrong with this reality, and I want you to really understand this—each dimensional reality serves a purpose, and each one is necessary to experience the other. From a spiritual vantage point, third-dimensional reality can be viewed as a necessary one because it is the doorway to other realities. Viewed this way, it is seen as a gift. Third-dimensional reality allows you to realize who you truly are through expanded consciousness.

It is the human experience to have emotional ups and downs in this dimensional reality of awareness. We can experience feelings of competition, a sense that one is better than or less than others, a belief that only action produces desired results, and a need to control things that are beyond control. Keep in mind that these emotions and attachments are required for spiritual growth; these are the very things that can become catalysts for a shift in consciousness. They also serve another purpose: they offer you the gift of choice. Emotions offer you a palette of colors with which to paint your life, so to speak. You have to experience fear before you can become fearless. You have to experience some confusion before clarity. You have to experience being separate from others before you can experience the feeling of oneness. And before you can experience personal freedom, you have to experience attachments to people or material things.

Fourth-Dimensional Reality

Fourth-dimensional reality is the moment when you begin to question the beliefs you've had about yourself and life in general. This is the beginning of a paradigm shift. A paradigm is a set of beliefs or ideas one has about themselves. At this stage of awareness, one is expanding their point of view, beginning to drop old, limiting beliefs and becoming open to new ideas and more empowering concepts. You might become a voracious reader, wanting to expose yourself to a variety of points of view and greater understandings.

Self-forgiveness and the forgiveness of others come into play at this stage. You begin to understand that letting go of the past starts by releasing the emotions that have kept you tied to it. It's a liberating process, one that raises your vibrational frequency as layers of accumulated negative emotion are laid aside. Clarity is experienced through forgiveness, and as you engage the powerful spiritual faculty known as forgiveness, you shift your energy field ever so closer to sixth chakra consciousness, the seat of clarity.

As the past is viewed through expanded awareness, the realization of the present as reality comes to the forefront of one's consciousness. The future is seen as the mind construct that it is; nothing more, nothing less. In other words, there's no judgment about the present, only the observation or witnessing of it.

Fifth-Dimensional Reality

The clearing of energy within you during fourth-dimensional reality sets the stage for the next dimensional reality, fifth-dimensional reality. At this stage, you fully realize the reality of oneness. This is the experience of enlightenment that I talked about in the last section. This is superconsciousness, heightened and expanded awareness realized. Here you consciously merge your awareness with that of Source Energy's while still being able to experience the individual soul that is you. It's an experience of coming and going, a beautiful wave of individual consciousness that dissolves into oneness that is free to resurface or reemerge as an individual soul, all while being aware of your interconnectedness with all of life.

In fifth-dimensional reality you enter into the field of potential and possibility. Fifth-dimensional reality is the birthplace of miracles. It is the quantum field, also known as the spiritual realm. At this level of awareness, you are free to manifest on a conscious level, no longer held down by automatic negative thinking. Psychic abilities are honed and further developed as you become more conscious of these spiritual gifts. You operate from unconditional love because its reality is experienced directly; you feel it within you *as* you, you see it within everyone and everything, and you know it's all the same thing, the same universal energy manifesting itself as countless forms.

The great gift offered to you in fifth-dimensional reality is the gift of contrast. You are still able to experience the conditioned mind, but it no longer controls you or dictates your future. You are now free. Free energetically, free to choose, free to be your authentic self, and free to manifest the life you truly desire, all while being of service to others. Talk about having your cake and eating it too!

This is probably the biggest realization that comes from operating from the fifth dimension of awareness: You realize that your vibrational frequency is the most powerful thing you have to manifest your reality. Being in the awareness of pure consciousness or stillness, that field of nothingness, all things become possible. And because you are in a state of allowing or nonresistance, things can manifest quite quickly because you are free of emotions like doubt and uncertainty.

What also happens at this level of awareness is that you realize your psychic abilities have a conscious awareness of their own. By having cleared your energy field, you free abilities such as clairvoyance, telepathy, and precognition to express themselves spontaneously. Source Energy is within everything, and that includes your psychic abilities. Everything is realized as having or possessing consciousness.

Lighten Your Emotional Load

You do not need to add anything to your life to become enlightened. Rather, you must shed layers of emotions, let go of the burdens of the past, and be able to clearly look at any fear of the future in order to come into clarity. In the weeks following my shift I experienced a tremendous amount of insight, and one of those insights revealed to me came as a moving image on how to release negative emotion.

By visualizing the release of old emotions, you free yourself energetically, clearing up your energy field. The practice of using this type of visual imagery is liberating, self-empowering, and relieving. It's empowering because during the process you are proactively taking steps to unburden yourself of anything that is no longer serving you, such as anger or guilt, which are typically roadblocks to clarity.

What we're going to look at now is the moving imagery I just described as an exercise. By the end of the exercise, you will likely feel a great sense of relief, feeling lighter for having let go of some emotional weights. Keep in mind that this is a powerful tool, one that can help liberate you, empower you, and give you the emotional relief you are deserving of.

• Emotional Release Exercise •

Remember, when you are visualizing the release of emotions, be mindful that it's happening in real time—not at some point in the future, but now, in the present. You should also be able to feel the difference in your energy field by doing a "before" and "after" contrast check, which I will give you within the exercise. Let's begin.

1. Get into a comfortable meditation position. Preferably, your spine is straight, your head is erect, and you are relaxed and in a state of allowing.

2. Take a moment or two and just rotate your arms. Take note of the weight of them and the energy around them and around your shoulders.

3. Close your eyes and follow your breaths for thirty seconds or so, allowing for deeper relaxation.

4. When you start feeling more relaxed, I want you to clear your mind and then imagine yourself standing on a grassy field. The sun is shining and the outside temperature is perfect.

5. Next, imagine a wooden crate is next to you. The lid is off. Take any negative emotion you've been feeling (such as anger, frustration, fear, or guilt) or any negative past experience and place these emotions into the crate. You can imagine these emotions as words or bags with the word "anger," "guilt," etc., written on them.

6. Once you've spent a minute or two placing these emotions into the crate, imagine the lid being placed on the crate. Chains automatically wrap around the crate on all sides, and the chain is then secured with a big lock.

7. Here is where you can get a little creative. It is time to release the crate filled with negative emotions. Perhaps you imagine yourself pushing the crate away from you, or you imagine the secured crate being put on a plane that takes off. You can even imagine the crate lifting off the ground and moving toward the sky, only to then be absorbed by the all-consuming power of the sun. Release the crate in a way that feels right to you.

8. Give thanks for the emotional release. Then take a few breaths and let the imagery go. Open your eyes, take another deep breath, and release it fully.

9. Take a moment to rotate your arms again. How do they feel? Do you feel a sense of lightness? Do you feel lighter on an energetic level? I am willing to guess that you do.

To start off, practice this exercise once or twice a week. It only takes a few minutes each time. As you clear your energetic field, you will find that this exercise is needed less and less. Once you're operating with greater clarity, you may find this exercise is only needed on occasion. Once you've become clearer on an energetic level, you will know when you feel the heaviness of negative emotion.

A Glimpse into the Quantum Field

My intention for this book has been to introduce higher-dimensional realities and expanded awareness concepts while making them as approachable, understandable, and practical as possible, and I will continue to do so in this section on the quantum field. The quantum field is just another descriptive phrase for the fifth dimension or the unmanifested spiritual realm. It's the field of pure awareness.

The quantum field is the field of awareness that you enter when the third eye is activated. It is the unrecognized, unknown, and unmanifested field where every possibility resides. It is unbound awareness; it's where all things become possible. This is where your spiritual self is found: in the field of enlightenment. And it's the awareness that you're already home, the experience of heaven on earth.

At this level of conscious awareness, perfection is seen in all things, even challenges, because one sees Source Energy in all things. And what I mean by the word perfection is that one comes from a point of view that all is well, that nothing is wrong, and that everything is working out for your highest good. To further clarify, this viewpoint sets the tone for your future life experiences; it allows for goodness to come into your life.

The last thing I want to say about the quantum field is that you're already operating within it; you just have to expand your awareness to its reality. By doing so, you come into greater alignment with your spirituality, your authentic self. The gift that comes with enlightenment is that you can experience all levels of reality (third, fourth, and fifth) simultaneously while being anchored in awareness of who you really are. Life becomes a beautiful painting filled with contrast.

I want to share with you ten insights that are expressions from the quantum field. Feel the energy of the words being offered. If they resonate with you, allow them to guide you to even greater understandings by reflecting on them, because what you focus on is what becomes your reality.

Ten Quantum Field Insights

1. The quantum field is here and now.
2. This field of awareness is found in inner stillness.
3. You are never separated from the quantum field.
4. The quantum field is a blank canvas, and you can re-create yourself and choose a new future from it.
5. When one reaches the enlightened state, one is operating consciously from pure awareness.
6. If you are in the quantum field consciously, you're going to experience personal freedom and soul expression.
7. The quantum field is where you will directly experience Source Energy as unconditional love, peace, clarity, wisdom, and understanding.
8. Intuition, telepathy, and your other psychic abilities are incredibly enhanced in this field of expanded awareness.
9. Gratitude and appreciation are gateways to this field; they open doors to possibility.
10. Oneness is the primary experience, but you are also able to experience yourself as an individual self.

chapter nine
WAYS TO ACTIVATE THE SIXTH CHAKRA

There are many ways to activate the sixth chakra because there are many ways to raise your vibrational frequency. The Challenge Negative Thinking Exercise and the Inner Stillness Meditation are excellent starting points to get you on your way to chakra activation, and they are also great at maintaining the sixth chakra's balance. In this chapter I offer several exercises, practices, and meditation techniques to assist you in creating greater momentum toward sixth chakra consciousness. Every action has something to offer you because each one is an extension of clarity and wisdom emanating from higher-dimensional levels of awareness. Because of the high vibration being offered through the written word, they have transformative power when allowed to resonate with your conscious awareness. In other words, shift happens.

Merge Mind, Body, and Soul

In this section we're going to look at how to merge your three aspects, what it's like to be in this three-in-one awareness, and the things that knock you out of alignment. I'll also offer you some tips on how to shift back into this awareness. To be clear, it's fairly easy to get into alignment and it's fairly easy to get out of it; it's all a matter of attention. The coming and going of your awareness is a practice of balance.

Consciously unifying the three aspects of your being is a powerful way to raise your vibrational frequency, and it's all a matter of alignment and awareness. What you become conscious of or aware of is what you come to experience. The mind, body, and soul are already one. Now move into that awareness. Acknowledge the soul as your innermost self, the mind as the awareness you use to be conscious of the soul, and the body as the vessel that allows you to interact with this world.

Being in spiritual alignment looks like being centered. You are not dispersing your vital life energy over challenging circumstances or undesired situations. You are focused on responding rather than reacting, which is what people are conditioned to do. It takes practice, but habits are learned, and through practice you can learn to be energetically centered, unifying all aspects of yourself. The simple phrase "go with the flow" best describes mind-body-spirit alignment.

Being in a state of resistance and finding things to complain about is what keeps most people out of alignment. Resistance to the outside world is what takes you out of your centeredness and into a space of scattered energy and focus; not very empowering. As for complaining, it lowers your vibrational frequency, bumping you out of spiritual awareness and back into third-dimensional awareness. But the good news is, that can be a temporary experience. With redirection and focus you can consciously make the shift back to alignment.

Here are some simple tips to help you shift into alignment and help you stay there:

- Find things to be thankful for.
- Cultivate an appreciative mindset.
- Discover what inspires you.
- Be creative.
- Set goals.
- Try to use all three of your aspects equally: move the body daily and breathe.
- Practice living through the awareness of the present moment.
- Meditate and set intentions to keep the mind focused.
- Pay attention to intuition and allow inspiration to flow through you.

In other words, it's important to express yourself. By doing so you free up stagnant, bottled-up energy and automatically bring all aspects into alignment. There's nothing more powerful than when mind, body, and spirit operate in unison.

Meditate

Meditation is the practice of focused yet relaxed awareness. Tuning in to the subtle energy body through this practice brings you into alignment with sixth chakra consciousness, allowing for intuition, clarity, and wisdom to flow. For some, guided visual imagery may be most beneficial for raising their vibrational frequency. Others may find that chanting helps them focus, thereby bringing them closer to higher-dimensional frequencies. And for others, the Inner Stillness Meditation is what works best for them. It all depends on where you're at in your spiritual journey. Some people may benefit from practicing all three of these versions of meditation. You could also look into wakeful meditation, where you live through great spiritual awareness and higher-dimensional consciousness moment by moment. Wakeful meditation can become second nature over time.

Let us now look at some different meditations. Though they differ in action, they all have the same goal, and that is to raise your vibrational frequency and shift you closer toward your deepest self. If you find yourself drawn to a specific meditation, that's perfectly fine.

• Guided Visual Imagery Meditation •

1. Get into a comfortable meditation position. Preferably, your spine is straight, your head is erect, and you are relaxed and in a state of allowing.

2. Close your eyes and follow your breaths for a few moments, allowing for deeper relaxation.

3. When you start feeling more relaxed, bring your awareness to the sixth chakra, just between your eyebrows, about a half inch above them.

4. Begin to visualize the color of the sixth chakra, indigo. It can be visualized in a shape of an eye or as a ball of light. Visualize this color for five minutes, imagining an indigo light being emitted from your sixth chakra. As you do this,

become aware of the energy around the chakra. Are there any vibrational sensations?

5. After five minutes have passed, release the image, take a deep breath, and open your eyes. Give thanks.

This meditation can be practiced daily. It is a powerful practice because it's one of intention. It signals to the sixth chakra that not only are you aware of its existence, but that you are choosing to be aligned with it in consciousness. Like any meditation practice, it should be approached without expectation. Instead of expecting something out of a meditation, be in a state of allowing, a space where anything is possible.

• Chanting Meditation •

1. Get into a comfortable meditation position. Preferably, your spine is straight, your head is erect, and you are relaxed and in a state of allowing.

2. Close your eyes and follow your breaths for a few moments, allowing for deeper relaxation.

3. Bring your awareness to the sixth chakra. Take a deep breath and exhale for five to seven seconds with the chant OM. Continue to do this with each exhalation for ten to fifteen minutes. The chant should be slow and controlled. If you are doing this correctly, you'll feel vibrations throughout your facial muscles during the chant. Your jaw should be slightly relaxed so there is no contact between the upper and lower teeth.

4. As you are chanting, become aware of the energy in and around your body. The subtle energy body will be felt as waves of vibrational energy.

5. After ten to fifteen minutes, take a deep breath and let go of the moment with gratitude. Practice this meditation once or twice a week.

A chakra mantra during meditation can have tremendous effects. The chant OM (or AUM) is one of the most common sixth chakra chants. It helps tune your vibration to sixth chakra consciousness by clearing old or lower-vibrating energies that are no longer serving you.

A key thing to remember about guided visual imagery or chanting is that you don't have to spend a lot of time doing these meditations to receive tremendous benefits. Less is more.

Release the Past

One of the most powerful and transformative practices you can employ to align yourself with sixth chakra consciousness is the mindful releasing of the past. By releasing the past, you come to experience a more empowered and enlightened future through the now. Our thoughts, emotions, and imagination are what open the door to our reality. In other words, all experience begins and ends with the mind. We're now going to discuss why you need to release the past, how to release it, and how doing so will accelerate your journey to sixth chakra activation.

The past—and the future, for that matter—are mental constructs. You can only experience them through your mind because that is where you've created them. The past only arrives in the now. The future only arrives in the now. Think about it. Reflect on these last two statements and then come to your own conclusions. These two constructs are based in third-dimensional consciousness, and as long as they are embraced, they will remain the chains that keep you from experiencing higher dimensions of consciousness.

Just to be clear, you are sacrificing nothing by letting go of the past as you reach for higher consciousness. You see, the gift in sixth chakra activation is that you can still experience multiple dimensions of consciousness, including the past and future, but the difference is that you are no longer attached to them. You are free, no longer in that dreaming state. And because you are free, you can experience these constructs through a deep awareness and see these third-dimensional thought forms for what they truly were: catalysts for your awakening.

The following spiritual exercise came to me in a vision shortly after my chakra activated. It is powerful and quite healing as well. After all, all emotional healing is a release of the past and the future. This exercise is one where the conscious mind is utilized to impress your intention upon the universal mind, thereby coming into alignment with what you desire.

• Release the Past Guided Meditation •

1. Find a quiet spot and get comfortable. Close your eyes and take a few slow breaths. Try to clear your mind by becoming aware of the present moment.

2. When you feel calm and relaxed, imagine yourself sitting in a room. The two halves of the room are separated by a blue line. You are on one side of the room. On the other side of the room is the word *past*.

3. Imagine having a brief conversation with your past. You can speak from the heart or say something along these lines:

"Thank you for being my catalyst. Thank you for the experiences. Thank you for the contrast. But where I am going, you cannot come. I release you and let go of you. My past will no longer dictate my future. I am free."

4. When you're done conversing and letting the past go, imagine yourself getting up and walking out of the room, away from the past. Close the door and allow yourself to feel liberated.

5. Take a deep breath and let the moment go. Open your eyes and give thanks that the past can no longer dictate your future.

This guided meditation can be done once a week or until you feel you no longer need it. You may find that after some practice with this particular meditation, you'll no longer require it because you've become conscious and aware when the past attempts to pull you back.

This meditation can also be done for the future, where you imagine the same scenario but instead are sitting across from the word *future*. Your conversation with the future might sound something like this: "My future will not be dictated by worry or fear. I am calling forth my daily experiences through gratitude and appreciation. Everything always works out for me. I am allowing wonderful and amazing things to manifest in my future through the present moment. There are miracles awaiting me."

Keep in mind that the ego may resist this practice because it is a way to break its hold on your consciousness. It wants to keep you in third-dimensional awareness because that is where it draws its power from. Let your ego throw all the tantrums it wants; just observe them. Fear nothing. Realize that you are the light and there is no darkness that can ever extinguish it.

This practice does two things simultaneously: it weakens the ego and its third-dimensional reality while strengthening the spiritual awareness (visualization, imagery) of the conscious mind. In other words, the releasing of the constructs of past and future is what allows you to raise your vibrational frequency, thereby bringing you closer to sixth chakra consciousness.

Be Authentic

For me, authenticity is an awareness of who I am beyond my ego and then expressing myself through that awareness as honestly as I possibly can. It's being unafraid of who I am and allowing every part of me, including my spiritual strengths and human limitations, to unfold spontaneously without resistance. Now, spontaneity is a word with some weight behind it. It is the perfect way to describe the soul because the soul isn't bound by the thinking mind; it exists beyond it. So being in a space of spontaneity is tantamount to living through the soul, allowing its expression.

Being authentic aligns you ever closer to your highest self. It's a vibration that removes barriers or any self-created blockages. I have found that authenticity makes people more approachable and more attractive on an energetic level. Because there is no resistance in this way of being, things manifest and seem to fall into people's laps, sometimes even before the desire or intention is placed.

Traits of Authentic People

There are many traits and qualities of truly authentic people. I'm going to list several here. You're probably going to find that you already have many, if not all, of these traits and qualities. You may find that you have these traits in varying degrees. Nevertheless, if you find yourself lacking in a particular trait, don't fret. Know that any of these traits can be cultivated through mindfulness.

- **They love and accept themselves unconditionally.** Because authentic people operate from the awareness that love is the only reality, they see the futility in hate and other lower-vibrating energies. They know that their power is based in self-love because love is what they are. They understand on a deep level that it's only through self-love and acceptance that they can extend the same to all others.

- **They are self-contemplative.** Often spending time looking within, one of their goals is to understand themselves on a deep level. Because of that, authentic people tend to be able to understand others because they realize oneness. Operating through higher levels of awareness, they are able to see the bigger picture, who they are and who everyone else is, in this miracle we call life.

- **They live in the moment.** Authentic people consciously choose not to live in the past, where their outlook can be darkened through negative emotion. Nor do they limit themselves by daydreaming about the future. They understand that all their power and strength is based in the now. They realize the fleeting nature of this life experience and seek to make the most out of every moment.

- **They go with the flow.** They are harmonious in nature, seeing detours where others see obstacles. Authentic people look deeply at adversity and see the lessons in it so that they can continue to grow spiritually. They are true alchemists, turning problems into opportunities.

- **They express themselves.** Being creative, authentic people heed the call of the soul. Whether they're artists, writers, designers, or bakers, these people realize that being comes before the doing. In other words, they know the joy that comes from being and then extend that to doing what they love.

- **They see unity.** Experiencing interconnectedness with all of life, authentic people see everything and everyone as a part of themselves. From this awareness they freely extend kindness and goodwill to all others. They are operating beyond the idea of separation, coming from a space of oneness.

- **They know anything is possible.** Having made the shift from limiting beliefs to the field of quantum possibility, authentic people don't align with limitations. They see the potential in virtually everything and allow for miracles to take place in their lives.

- **They are thoughtful.** They consider others' feelings and points of view. Knowing this is a world of contrast, they respect and see great value in others' perspectives. They see others as channels for divine wisdom and insight.

- **They forgive and forget.** Understanding the releasing power of forgiveness, authentic people readily extend it to others. Because they operate from higher-frequency vibrations, they choose not to dwell on past trespasses. Instead, they remain focused on the present.

- **They choose happiness.** Because authentic people have experienced lower-vibrating emotions and realized the futility in remaining in those frequencies, happiness and contentment become conscious choices. They simply think or say "I am happy," all while knowing the power in their thoughts and words.

Use Affirmations

You have a very powerful, life-changing tool at your disposal: the conscious mind. The conscious mind is a reflection of the higher dimensions of consciousness within you. And it's the ideal weapon of choice to challenge low-vibrating emotions. In this section you're going to learn how to use it and focus it to set intentions that activate the third eye.

Before I offer some affirmations, allow me to discuss the power of the phrase "I am." When you start an intention with the words "I am," you start the powerful engine of the universal mind. Notice that the phrase is in present tense; it is not "I was" or "I will be." The universe operates now, in this one holy, wholly instant. What words you say after "I am" is what sets universal forces in motion, and you must have faith.

Here are some intentions that are directly and indirectly affirming.

- I am awakened now.
- I am experiencing sixth chakra activation.
- I am free.
- I am transcendent.
- I am beyond the five senses.

- I am transformed.
- I am whole and complete.
- I am one with everything.
- I am focused.
- I am one in mind, body, and spirit.
- I am trusting the process.
- I am fearless.
- I am peace.
- I am wisdom.
- I am clarity.
- I am what Source Energy says I am.
- I am understanding.
- I am joy.
- I am strength.
- I am living through my highest self.

These are just a few examples of some very powerful intentions. The key is to affirm them as being true now, regardless of past thinking and experience. The sixth chakra operates from the dimension of limitless possibility and potential; it has no ties whatsoever to human conditioning, like the past or future. Your highest self operates independently from this world.

These affirmations can be expressed throughout the day. Repetition has a way of building momentum because everything is energy and there is great force behind the spoken word. As you are in the process of manifesting, remember to remain nonattached to outcomes. This goes for any desire; set the intention, practice gratitude, develop your faith and trust, and let go. The vibrational frequency of impatience and frustration will only give you more and more of the same.

Trust That You Are Guided

I have found that most people, at one point or another, have been spontaneously inspired to take action or have intuitively become aware of something about to happen. A common theme throughout these accounts is that something beyond themselves—a higher energy, so to speak—grabbed their attention, showing them the way or revealing something they could not have known otherwise. These positive, higher-frequency energies or beings can be described as guides, angels, loved ones who have passed, ascended masters, or enlightened beings, just to name a few.

These spiritual guides are always nearby, ready to offer assistance and provide insight, especially when called on. Sometimes they come as intuition, a soft telepathic thought, or full-on energetic warnings. The first step in receiving guidance is to be mindful that spirit guides are with you and always ready to offer assistance. The next step is to practice active listening, which is an exercise in adjusting your focus or tuning in to sixth chakra consciousness by employing some of the techniques I discussed earlier, such as living in the present and meditating upon inner stillness. The channel to receive divine wisdom and guidance is just beyond the five senses in the frequency of a quieted mind.

As you continue to raise your vibrational frequency through conscious practices, you'll find that the guidance becomes clearer. You can even connect with your spirit guides through quiet meditation. It's important to be in a good space energetically and to have no expectations for how communication will take place or if it will take place on the first try. This is because spirit guides are operating at an incredibly high frequency, and it's important that your vibrational frequency be high as well in order to discern their message.

On occasion, I have consciously connected with my guides. The one who always comes through the strongest and clearest is Holy Mother Mary. Each and every time I have focused within and asked, "Who are my guides?" I received in the gentlest, most beautiful female energy, "Mary" before I could even finish asking. Nothing more needed to be said; I understand exactly who she is. Your guides want to assist you in any way they can, and the following story is an example of that.

One morning a few years back, I was driving to work. I was downtown, driving toward the dental office where I worked. I began driving up a three-lane winding hill that was somewhat like a highway with a speed limit of forty-five miles per hour. By the time I approached the first wide curve, I suddenly realized that I was driving over fifty miles per hour and still accelerating. Before I completed the curve and entered the straightaway, I received a telepathic message that said, "Cop ahead." I immediately took my foot off the gas. Sure enough, there was a speed trap waiting for me just under the upcoming bridge. Thankfully, I heeded the spiritual warning, and by the time I approached the police officer I was driving the speed limit, averting a speeding ticket. This is just one example of my spirit guides offering assistance.

Be Aware of the Subtle Body

The subtle body, or energy body, houses the chakras. It's an extension of the soul and its frequency can be perceived by raising your vibrational frequency through focused, quiet meditation. Becoming aware of the subtle body and experiencing its waves of healing energy will only accelerate sixth chakra activation through conscious alignment. By healing energy, I mean the subtle body's ability to clear out low-vibrating energy because it is based in unconditional love. Awareness of this higher-frequency body is the basis for energy medicine or energy healing. Consciously tuning in to this energy body balances the chakras and potentially creates the perfect atmosphere for spontaneous sixth chakra awakening and healing. The following meditative exercise is going to focus on increasing your awareness of the subtle body through direct experience.

• Tuning In Exercise •

1. Find a quiet spot and get comfortable. Close your eyes and follow your breaths for a few moments, allowing for deeper relaxation.

2. Clear your mind through present moment awareness and start by bringing your awareness to your head and forehead area. Allow yourself to become acutely aware of every sensation. Feel the universal life force animating every cell in your scalp, forehead, and facial muscles. Sense your ears. Sense your lips and cheeks. Feel the aliveness flowing through you. As you tune in to the energy supply within, you will find you are experiencing waves of energy surrounding your head. This is the subtle body.

3. After five or ten minutes, move on to your shoulders, arms, hands, and then fingers. Again, feel the energy emanating from within and surrounding your physical body. Continue this for five or ten minutes.

4. Move your awareness to your upper body: your chest, back, and abdominal area. Continue to be focused on body awareness, resisting no thoughts as you allow them to pass.

5. After a few minutes, allow your awareness to flow toward your hips, buttocks, and reproductive center. Allow the universal energy to flow through you as you continue to surrender your awareness to the subtle body.

6. After five or ten minutes, bring your awareness to your legs, then your feet.

7. After a few more minutes, bring your awareness to gratitude for all that your body does for you as a vessel. Give thanks for its healing power to restore and maintain balance.

8. For the last few minutes, allow your awareness to travel freely throughout your body, feeling the subtle body as a whole while allowing yourself to experience feelings of deep relaxation, peace, and calm.

9. Bring your awareness back to your surroundings, open your eyes, and give thanks for the experience.

This exercise can range between twenty-five to fifty minutes in length, depending on your level of comfort and desire. It can be practiced once or twice a week, depending on what works for you. Once you've mastered the focused concentration of tuning in to the subtle body, you'll be able to shift into it instantly, virtually at will.

The benefits of this practice are a deeper sense of calm and inner peace, a greater ability to deal with everyday stresses, increased alignment with your highest self and chakra systems, and a greater sense of clarity, not only in a spiritual sense but also in regard to what the body requires.

Be Aware of Energetic Blockages

As you begin to experience higher levels of consciousness, you may find that you occasionally are hitting a plateau. A plateau will usually come in the form of an energy blockage that has been stirred up as you've cultivated the mind. The key to getting unstuck during these temporary phases is to become aware of them and identify them. I have found that a common energy blockage faced by those on the spiritual path is a lack of self-forgiveness or forgiveness of others. In other words, a very common energy that needs to be faced and released is guilt.

Practicing self-forgiveness and forgiveness of others is a powerful exercise in raising your vibrational frequency. It is quite possibly the most effective exercise you could ever employ. Forgiveness has the potential to free you of things gone by, thereby clearing your mind of the slings and arrows coming from the past. There is great strength in forgiveness, and because of that, it's transformative. Do not underestimate forgiveness's ability to literally change your life's direction. It's that potent.

As for other energetic blockages, they usually appear as a negative emotion that simply hasn't been addressed and dealt with. Your goal, then, is to recognize the emotion that is presenting itself to you. Try the following exercise.

• Energetic Blockage Clearing Exercise •

1. Identify the emotion. Is it past or future based? The past usually has feelings of sadness, regret, and guilt. The future often comes with fear, worry, and anxiety.

2. Separate yourself from the thought or emotion. Observe it through nonreaction. Recognize the negative thought or

emotion for what it is: an illusion, a dream, the playing out of the unconscious ego self.

3. You may notice that as you do so, you're becoming aware of a presence within; that's your highest self. As your negative emotion is being starved through nonreaction, you're allowing the expansion of your own consciousness and the blossoming of the third eye.

4. As you're observing the negative emotion, come up with a positive or conscious thought to replace it. Doing this activates the force of the sixth chakra and may cause a spontaneous activation.

5. Consciously let go of the negative emotion. If it returns, continue with the same conscious practice until that particular blockage has lost all energy. Remember: starve the ego, feed your soul.

Use this exercise as needed.

chapter ten

WHAT TO EXPECT AS YOU APPROACH THIRD EYE ACTIVATION

During the months prior to my sixth chakra activation, I noticed that I was more irritable than usual. I also constantly had the feeling that something was going to happen soon. Looking back, it would have been beneficial to have some insight as to what was happening because it was a very confusing time for me. With that being said, I am going to share some sensations and experiences you may encounter as you journey toward activation.

If You Are Approaching Activation, You May Have...

- **Pressure in the forehead or between the eyebrows.** Several months or weeks before brow chakra activation, you may find that you're feeling pressure or a slight vibrating feeling in the center of your forehead. This is a signal that the third eye is preparing to open. The moment of activation provides instant clarity.

- **A greater feeling of uneasiness.** Something I have learned about circumstances is that they aren't always what they seem. As I approached the moment of awakening, I began to experience deeper and darker emotions. Looking back, it was an experience in emotional contraction, just before expansion of consciousness.

- **Experiences in indigo or violet.** The colors associated with the sixth chakra are indigo and violet, and as you get closer to activation you may experience spontaneous visual bursts of this color. Before activation they signal upcoming change. Post-activation, occasional color bursts are a sign of a balanced chakra.

- **More frequent headaches.** Before chakra activation you may experience an increase in tension headaches. This is most likely due to an increase in spiritual energy as the chakra is about to activate (and then activate all others through your spine). The energy travels upward and springs forth through the activating brow chakra. Another way to describe it would be contraction, contraction, contraction, followed by release.

- **Feelings of a greater oneness with life.** As you're moving past limiting emotions and beliefs, you are simultaneously raising your vibrational frequency. This causes greater clarity and more direct experiences of unity. In other words, less ego identification equals less feelings of separation.

- **New experiences with sound and light.** You may find that colors are appearing more vivid than before. This may happen before and after chakra activation. Senses become heightened overall, and you may experience some temporary sensitivity to sounds as you adjust to greater levels of awareness.

- **Increased psychic senses.** Heightened intuition, clairvoyance, and overall extrasensory perception may be experienced as you come closer and closer to the seat of wisdom and clarity.

Becoming Superconscious

Some of you may have heard of the term *superconscious*, which is why I feel it should be addressed. There are differences between the superconscious and subconscious minds. The subconscious is just below conscious awareness; it's a storage system for all that you are not conscious of. The superconscious mind has no boundaries and brings insight, potential, and creativity to conscious awareness. Simply put, the superconscious is the hyperawareness of the highest self and the consciousness that is a reflection of it. In other words, this state beyond all states is the merging of individual consciousness into that of The All That Is. Walls of separation are taken down and you receive the keys to the mansion, so to speak, opening the door to limitless possibilities.

In superconscious awareness all senses are heightened, both physical and nonphysical. For example, hearing becomes almost supernatural due to the clarity and inner silence experienced moment by moment. Psychic abilities that you were aware of develop even further through the activated chakra, and abilities that you were unaware of begin to express themselves spontaneously.

Operating through superconscious awareness also comes with an adjustment phase. In this awareness you sense things that most cannot and you see things most don't. I'll give you an example. A few years ago I was visiting a friend over the holidays. My friend's house was a few doors down from the corner. There was no parking available in front of his house this particular winter evening, so I had to park around the corner. As I walked to my friend's house, I admired the house on the corner and its big, beautiful windows, including a large, rounded window where the Christmas tree lights beamed through the glass. It was a beautiful sight.

After a few hours of laughing, talking about cars, and eating pizza, I left my friend's house and began to walk back to my car. As I approached the house on the corner, something caught my attention on an energetic level, and I turned around to see what I felt. As my eyes were drawn to the window where the Christmas tree was, I was astonished to see a shadow figure looking into the window. It appeared to be mesmerized by all the lights. It was darker than the area surrounding it, standing maybe five and a half feet in height. I was only granted a few seconds of observation because the moment the paranormal entity noticed me, it vanished into the darkness. I stopped in my tracks for a few seconds, contemplating what I had just witnessed.

Reflecting back on this experience, hindsight tells me a few things. It was my awareness of this shadow figure that sent it packing. And my response to it, witnessing it through awareness and not fear, is what closed the door to any attachment. This, by the way, wasn't the last time that I was able to perceive paranormal phenomena. I will share some more examples in chapter 11.

The purpose of this section was to give you some insight and a spiritual heads-up to some of the things you can expect as you become superconscious from within, which will then automatically extend to the world around you.

Operating from Multiple Dimensions

Throughout the day you engage in various levels of awareness or dimensions of consciousness. Perhaps you experience sadness one moment and joy the next. It happens when you're confused and looking for an answer and then find it later on through inspiration or a stroke of genius. You experience multiple dimensions when you've become angry at your partner and then choose to forgive them. The goal here is twofold; first, it's to make you aware that you're tuning in to multiple dimensions of consciousness each and every day. The second goal is to have you become more aware when you're experiencing those higher dimensions of consciousness. Keep in mind that I use the word *higher* as a relative term. In truth, no one dimension is better than another. Higher is the best term to describe the frequency, which is lighter, and it gives you the bigger picture. You see yourself and the world around you from beyond the ego. It's as if the ego and its thought process are the clouds and your elevated awareness is what raises you above them in order to observe them with greater understanding, thereby understanding yourself and others more effectively.

Here are some telltale signs that you're connecting with higher dimensions of consciousness, thereby coming into greater alignment with your spiritual self and sixth chakra consciousness:

• You're quicker to forgive—but not only that, you're forgetting, releasing what no longer serves you, which in this case is guilt.

- You're becoming more compassionate and extending it to others frequently.
- There is a greater feeling of lightness to your vibrational frequency.
- You're seeing life's beauty and sacredness.
- Inner peace is becoming more of a priority for you.
- You are choosing happiness more often through conscious choice; you are not waiting for outside circumstances to change.
- Manifesting consciously is becoming a greater part of your experience.
- You're enjoying your moments of solitude.
- You're seeing the divine in everything and everyone.
- Inner stillness is being experienced through meditation, the most telltale sign there is.

Telepathy Is the Glue

It's no coincidence when you think of someone and then receive a text, email, or phone call from that person. Through oneness, we are all connected. This connection does not stop here on Earth; you are infinitely connected to everything and everyone throughout the universe. Being an extension of Source Energy, there are no limits put upon you; that includes the ability to communicate with the living and with those who have transitioned to the afterlife.

Telepathy is just another form of energy transmission and interpretation through the unseen energy circuit pathways that connect us all. It is thought transference between two things; between people, plants, or animals, or between a person and some other-dimensional being—this could be a spirit guide, an ascended master, or a loved one who passed.

The phenomenon of telepathy seems to be more likely between those who have had strong relationships, like siblings, parents, or partners. The reason for that is we tend to think of these people more often, and where attention goes, energy flows. I cannot tell you how many times I have been talking about or thinking of a sibling only to have one of them suddenly touch base with me. I am certain many people have had similar experiences.

Mediums have learned to focus and clear their channel for this type of communication. They can receive communication through thoughts, feelings, or images. This ability to clearly receive information beyond the five senses is based in oneness. If oneness is an all-encompassing reality, then telepathy is the glue within that oneness that keeps things together or connected. You can strengthen your telepathic abilities and simultaneously move closer to sixth chakra activation through a simple technique. Before you attempt telepathy, though, there are a few ways to prepare.

Preparing for Telepathy

- The art of receiving: Practice relaxation techniques like quiet meditation. Messages or impressions are more easily received in a relaxed state because through this focused awareness, clarity is greatly increased.

- The art of sending: This simply requires focus. Practice sending a message either as an image, thought, or emotion. The goal is to be clear in what you're sending; clear your mind of any distractions as you send your message. This makes it easier for the receiver to interpret the message. Lastly, be aware of how powerful of an imprint thoughts, emotions, and intentions make in the quantum field.

• Contemplate oneness: For a few minutes a day, contemplate your oneness with everyone and everything. When you observe the world around you, be aware that consciousness is all-encompassing and that we're all connected through oneness and the glue of telepathy.

• Telepathic Exercise •

One of the best ways to further develop your telepathic abilities is to practice sending and receiving messages. Practice with a friend. Remember that distance is of no consequence in the spirit realm, as all is one and all is now.

1. If you're going to be the sender first, get into a relaxed state and then choose a word, thought, image, or emotion. Send it telepathically by focusing on your friend. See if they pick up on it.

2. When it is your turn to be the receiver, continue your relaxed state to allow for greater clarity. Focus your attention on the sender. See if you are picking up on any words, thoughts, images, or emotions.

Keep in mind that the ultimate goal here is greater clarity, which will lead to increased awareness, which will allow you to pick up on psychic messages more easily in your everyday life.

This exercise can be performed weekly for fifteen to thirty minutes.

The Spirit World Is Here and Now

To clearly understand the world and our place in it, we need to look at life with greater clarity. Human beings have been programmed to believe that there is life and then death, but really there is only life and *more* life, eternal. Those of you on the spiritual path have probably read about this world and the spirit world as if they are separate. Because people are experiencing contrast in this life—dark and light; the past, the now, and the future—we can lose sight of where we really are.

I'm going to start by taking away the power that death has in many people's minds. Understandably, death can be fear-inducing, but to know what death really is will empower you and you will lose all fear of it. Death is a shift in awareness. Death is release from physical limitations; it's the letting go and conquering of the ego so that your spiritual self can rise into your awareness. In other words, the ego must fall for the soul to rise. The ego is laid aside at the end of one's life. But this can also take place through sixth chakra activation or spiritual awakening. Ego death, then, is simply the shedding of fear, worry, depression, sadness, and any other limiting emotion or energy. This process of laying the ego aside so you can live through your spirit is what follows chakra activation. It's the lifting of the veil so you can see yourself and the unseen mechanics of life with perfect clarity.

Source Energy has countless attributes; it is eternal, changeless, the unseen, all-encompassing, limitless, and unconditional love. As extensions of Source Energy, we too share the same attributes and characteristics. And if oneness is a reality, then one must conclude that separation is an illusion. With that being said, we are led to question the reality of the known world relative to the spirit world. It all comes down to matter.

Matter is spirit or consciousness expressed outwardly. Everyone and everything—including this planet, this solar system, this universe, for that matter—is Source Energy expressing itself so that it can know itself experientially. In other words, the spirit world is here and now. You won't find it in the past and you won't recognize it through the future; it is right here, right now, in this one instant. That is the miracle of Source Energy, which is the miracle and mystery of life. The past and the future are happening in one moment, a miracle so unimaginable that words fail to describe what is taking place. Realizing this can't help but make one approach life with complete awe and wonderment.

The world of matter and the world of spirit are one. Take a look at matter closely and you will see that it's made up of molecules, atoms, and quarks. Keep going and what you're left with is space—everything is made up of 99.9 percent space.[1] What is this space? It's consciousness and it's self-aware. Which leads us to what we're all here on Earth to do: to become self-aware and to remember our true identity, our oneness with the universe, and then to demonstrate that inner knowing, which is made possible through the brow chakra.

Automatic Writing

I like to describe automatic writing as clear writing. It's a process where pen and paper (or hands and keyboard) and allowing through wakeful meditation meet. It's a psychic ability that in fact may be one of the simplest to master through intention and action. Besides that, it's an excellent way to tune in to

---

1. Ali Sundermier, "99.9999999% of Your Body Is Empty Space," *Business Insider Australia*, February 14, 2021, https://www.businessinsider.com .au/physics-atoms-empty-space-2016-9.

higher dimensions of consciousness by directing your focus. If you've never tried automatic writing before, you can start with some simple questions or a few different spiritual topics and see what's revealed by letting go and allowing divine wisdom to flow through you.

The great thing about the practice of automatic writing is that it involves the sixth chakra by engaging it as you channel higher-dimensional wisdom. I never realized it at the time, but automatic writing was something I always did when I had essays to write in English class. The essays used to flow from my fingertips with little effort. I would suspend the thinking mind and simply focus on the topic at hand, allowing clarity to direct my hand unknowingly. All of us experience this to some degree, but being aware of it when it's happening is the key. I'm going to offer you some direction and guidance that will not only help you in developing this incredible psychic ability, but will also move you along your journey toward chakra activation.

Automatic Writing Tips

- Try to work in a quiet space. Sometimes having quiet music playing in the background can help you become more relaxed.
- Spend a few minutes meditating on inner silence. This will prepare you by raising your vibrational frequency, thereby quieting the thinking mind so that you can focus on the wisdom being offered.
- Give thanks for the forthcoming information and acknowledge your spirit guides.
- Jot down a few spiritual topics or write down a few questions, then let go and allow.

- Keep the pen and paper (or keyboard) ready. Information downloads quite quickly at times.

- Surrender to wisdom and allow your pen (or your fingers on the keyboard) to be guided.

- Be patient. Trust the process. Practice and then practice some more. If automatic writing is something that you're really drawn to, then practice it several times a week, perhaps for fifteen to thirty minutes at a time.

- Try not to get frustrated when or if nothing happens. This happens to many automatic writers. Simply walk away and return to it later on or during a moment of inspiration.

Deeper Connections

The result of living authentically is that you become deeply aware and connected with your spiritual self. This relationship, when nurtured and deepened through trust, will then extend outwardly to others and the world around you. Operating through single vision or oneness via the third eye, you come to see and experience yourself as one with everything and everyone. There is no longer any separation, but unity. Fear is replaced with trust because you understand that what you fear you call forth, and by choosing trust instead, you're choosing a future that can be trusted.

To put it simply, you're deciding daily whether you live in a friendly or hostile world. It all comes back to your inner world and experience there. Understanding that an effect is the result of past thinking, you have the free will to choose differently. You're not bound to your past. You can change your future in the now. However, if one is operating from mostly third-dimensional consciousness, then the experience will most likely be one of projected fear or judgment, which is then returned in kind because what we see within is what's reflected outwardly. The good news is that this completely changes when operating through higher dimensions. Projection is replaced with extension. Love always extends; it gives. Fear is what always projects, causing contraction.

If you want to experience a deeper connection with life and with others, look no further than yourself. Return to your center and become reacquainted with your spiritual self. Let your energy flow. Remember what it was like being a child, free and without worry. Allow yourself to lighten up and let go of some seriousness. Make peace with yourself and allow that peace to flow outwardly. Practice the sacred art of forgiveness. Love yourself unconditionally despite all the supposed mistakes you've made; you are deserving of unconditional love because that is what you are. What if all your mistakes and missteps served a purpose? Would they still be viewed as mistakes, or would you see them as lessons on your journey to who you are destined to become? Imagine seeing your mistakes as blessings. What would you call them if they ultimately led you to greater insight and understanding, thereby bringing you closer to who you are below the surface?

Maintaining Balance

Many of us have probably heard the phrase "Life's all about balance." Let's look at what that really means, how balance is achieved, and what it has to do with the brow chakra. The first thing to understand is that balance is first achieved through inner action. When it's an inner experience, it will automatically become an outer one as well through conscious decision-making.

Balance really has to do with energy. The ego is responsible for automatic negative reactions, and your conscious mind has the duty to respond to those lower energies with higher-vibrating positive thoughts. Conscious positive thinking is what negates unconscious negative thinking. It makes perfect mathematical sense: -1 (negative thought) + 1 (positive thought) = 0. And the more you engage the conscious mind by responding to the slings and arrows of the egoic mind, the more positive energy you'll engage, all while diminishing the ego's hold on your consciousness.

This practice of engaging the conscious mind changes your inner experience because it balances the energies inside of you. Once that energy has been balanced over time through practice, clarity will be allowed to unfold more and more. Through clarity, you will witness just how valuable inner balance is. Inner clarity allows you to realize the importance of being self-centered—not in an egotistical way, but through the awareness that if you take care of yourself first, you can be of service to others much more effectively. Inner awareness ensures you are no longer a people pleaser. There is nothing wrong with being a people pleaser, but there is a fine line between helping others and stretching yourself so thin that you're left with no energy to do the things you want to do. In other words, it's a practice in self-responsibility.

Ultimately, we're each responsible for ourselves and our own happiness. When you place your happiness in someone else's hands, you give it away. No one can be responsible for the way you feel; it's an inside job. Besides, once you find true inner balance, you won't have the desire to place your happiness in another's hands because you can call it forth consciously by choosing it. This actually allows for better relationships because you are no longer expecting someone else to complete you; rather, you end up sharing your completeness. This ends up being a very empowering practice on so many levels. You will find you have greater energy levels because universal energy is now allowed to flow freely throughout your inner being with little to no emotional reaction impeding it. Time is no longer obsessed over because of your high degree of self-management. Life becomes simpler because you're operating from a place of inner power and inner balance.

A Treasure Trove of Spiritual Faculties

As you journey toward activating the sixth chakra, you may find that you are becoming more and more aware of your various psychic abilities. Even now, several years' post–chakra activation, I am becoming aware of other capabilities such as retrocognition. I have astounded friends and family members at times when I have had discussions with them and received impressions about the feelings they were experiencing at a particular point in the past.

With that being said, I feel it would be valuable to become more aware of what psychic abilities you're experiencing as you progress toward sixth chakra consciousness. Awareness is everything when it comes to living spiritually. I find it appropriate to identify and label what abilities are perhaps more developed than others to help you know your strengths and what abilities require further development should you decide to pursue them further. For example, I am aware what my psychic strengths are and know which ones I am drawn to.

Some psychic abilities are stronger than others; I feel that's based on an individual's life purpose. For example, a few years back I met a friend for coffee whom I hadn't seen in a while. Her father had just passed away and I had been out of the country when the funeral was held. As we sat there talking and sipping coffee, I suddenly got an image of a man that I felt was her father. I began to describe him to her: his physical stature, his facial features, what his hair looked like. I said, "He just wants you to know he's here and he's good." My friend sat there, kind of stunned and at a loss for words for a few moments. Then she smiled and expressed her elation about receiving the message. Even though I had never met her father, she remarked how accurate my description of him was.

Although I have the ability of mediumship as a result of sixth chakra consciousness, it's not necessarily my calling. I could teach mediumship and show others how to open themselves to direct communication, but working as a medium is not my life's purpose. I feel it's essential to follow one's path; heed the call, so to speak. My calling, which I feel as an inner knowing of my life's purpose, is that of a spiritual teacher. I reveal the infinite potential in consciousness and demonstrate to others how to connect to higher dimensions of consciousness so they can empower themselves and further develop their psychic abilities through sixth chakra activation.

If you have experienced psychic events in the past, take a moment and reflect on them. Were they experiences in clairvoyance or clairaudience? Do one or several abilities seem to shine through more than others? Does mediumship come easy to you? Honing your strengths and realizing where further development is needed can save you a lot of time and effort in realizing your life's purpose.

chapter eleven

PARANORMAL PHENOMENA AND PSYCHIC EVENTS

Awareness is a crucial element in developing any spiritual faculty, but it is often hindered by distraction, which in this case is the ego or conditioned mind. The ego works really hard to try to keep you in a sort of hypnotic trance, and it does this through the allure of past and future thinking. Its energy is addictive in nature because it is the very essence of attachment. People misidentify themselves as their ego because of its close proximity. You are not the ego; you are the awareness experiencing it. With that being said, you cannot help but feel your vibrational frequency and your awareness rise after taking a closer look at the ego.

Your true awareness is the silent witness within, the authentic you. It's consciousness, pure, all-knowing, and free of attachments. But you have to allow it to return to the forefront of your consciousness. In other words, you have to be conscious of your awareness.

Your directed awareness or consciousness is what creates your reality. Focusing on the egoic mind is what creates a third-dimensional reality experience. But allowing your inner awareness to come to mind and being mindful of the presence within is what allows a new reality to unfold through higher dimensions of consciousness. In other words, everything you desire (including heightened psychic abilities) is just beyond the ego.

Be aware of the transformative power of written words, especially when they're extensions of higher dimensions of consciousness. They have the potential to set off a spiritual chain reaction that can trigger a spontaneous awakening; I know this from experience. When allowed to resonate within you, high-vibrating information can ignite the deeper awareness in you and cause it to temporarily reveal ultimate reality in a powerful way, leading to a transcendent experience.

If you're operating from higher dimensions of consciousness, then you're spiritually aware and conscious of your eternal, unchanging, unconditionally loving self. It would be accurate to say that awareness changes everything because through awareness, you can consciously identify yourself with Source Energy through the clarity of that very awareness. And through heightened awareness, which is simply the expansion of your local consciousness, you can become further aware of spiritual tools and abilities you thought you never had. A process of rediscovery, it's like going on a treasure hunt within your very self, where treasures most certainly abound.

A moment of hyperawareness could trigger spontaneous sixth chakra activation. It could be that simple and direct. Indeed, the potential is always there. Desire and willingness are very important ingredients. There are no limits to consciousness, so let go of any thoughts about how or when activation is going to happen. This inner action allows the universe to express itself fully through you with perfect timing.

You have arrived on this planet lacking nothing except for the awareness of what you're already in possession of. What you must do is claim what's already yours. Know who you are spiritually. Realize that nothing has to be added to you. Awaken to the fact that you're already in the spiritual realm.

To recap, this is the one and only roadblock to fully realizing and expressing your psychic abilities: ego. It's the veil preventing you from seeing the reality of pure consciousness and the infinite potential within it. As extensions of Source Energy, we are already whole and complete; nothing is lacking in a spiritual sense. But we do have to grow in awareness and the understanding that we are more than the thinking mind and much, much more than flesh and bone.

You've always been guided. Now become aware of it. You've experienced moments of clarity. Now become aware of it. You've been understanding and compassionate. Now become aware of it. You've experienced moments of intuition. Now become aware of it. Stop second guessing yourself! Kick doubt to the curb and embrace the certainty of your inner being. All that you seek and desire is within.

Self-acceptance of who and what you are is how you love and honor yourself. It is the key to self-expression. Embracing the entirety of you—mind, body, and soul—is the secret to self-love and allowing that love to extend as your spiritual gifts. Acknowledging all aspects of the self is the path to self-realization. Your very self is one with Source and Source is your very self. Source Energy becomes what it creates. This unlimited power is not separate from creation; it is creation itself. Understanding this, you can see how lack of any kind in a spiritual sense is, well, impossible. Spiritually speaking, you are a perfect and complete being, but the temporary state of being human has convinced us otherwise. However, in realizing what we're not, we can fully experience and understand who and what we are. You have the tools: your psychic capabilities. They're just buried under layers of human conditioning. Dig deep within yourself and find them. Allow them to be expressed so you can become who you were meant to be.

The Two Worlds Are One

A little bit of clarity will go a long way in understanding that paranormal phenomena and the psychic world are actually intertwined. They occur most of the time without a person's conscious awareness, either through a lack of belief or due to everyday distractions. Paranormal phenomena and psychic events are often misunderstood, but they both serve a purpose: a soul purpose. More so, these two worlds reflect one another based on a person's level of awareness, and they are always personal experiences.

Everyone has some level of psychic ability, but not everyone believes in them. Not everyone realizes we live in a spiritual world. According to a 2005 survey, 41 percent of Americans believe in extrasensory perception (ESP), 31 percent believe in telepathy, 26 percent believe in clairvoyance, and 21 percent believe in mediumship.[2] Even if those who do not believe in psychic abilities were to experience them, they would not be consciously aware because the door has been shut on their possible existence. Everyone is telepathic, for example, but most simply aren't aware

---

2. David W. Moore, "Three in Four Americans Believe in Paranormal," Gallup, June 16, 2005, https://news.gallup.com/poll/16915/three-four -americans-believe-paranormal.aspx.

that they are. Everyone experiences moments of clairvoyance, but because of human conditioning, these events are dismissed or simply unacknowledged. The conditioned mind says, "Show me and I'll believe it," or, "It's just not possible." In other words, when someone is closed-minded, anything outside of their individual belief system simply cannot exist because to believe in anything else would threaten that belief system. Many people will never experience paranormal phenomena or psychic events because there is no possibility or awareness there, and where awareness goes, energy flows. Furthermore, even if an event were to happen, it most likely would be missed simply because the nonbeliever would be too caught up in third-dimensional consciousness.

Psychic abilities and paranormal phenomena are other-worldly in nature as they are other-dimensional. If one is operating strictly from third-dimensional consciousness, their vibrational frequency won't be tuned to the frequency where these abilities and phenomena exist and can be experienced. It all goes back to awareness. When the mind has been quieted and is still, awareness arises, allowing for unimaginable clarity: clear seeing, clear sensing, and so on. But if the mind is full of distractions, then those other-dimensional experiences will be almost impossible to perceive. Remember: awareness, awareness, awareness! It cannot be emphasized enough.

Misunderstanding can be experienced when some uncertainty or limiting beliefs are in play. There's a difference between knowing that you're being guided and thinking something's just a hunch. Knowing leads to clarity; in fact, it is where clarity is experienced. Belief is apt to change, but knowing simply is, and it cannot be argued with. If you've been wondering if you are being spiritually guided or have spirit guides, know that you are and you do. Making the shift—coming from a place of knowing rather than belief—

can be as simple as making a decision. But if you're not ready to make that decision just yet, meditate upon it. Meditate on your spirit guides, meditate upon the various psychic abilities, and allow understanding to guide you; you may be surprised at what's offered through just a little willingness in wanting to know more. Knowing is a powerful force as it opens the door to experience, invites possibility, and activates potential.

Ego Shadows

Having watched numerous paranormal programs, I have noticed a common misunderstanding. Oftentimes, investigators think they're communicating with the actual soul or spirit of a person. They don't realize that they're actually communicating with or experiencing the shadow of that person, the egoic shadow that has been left behind. Allow me to clarify. As beautiful as this world is, it's also a spiritual landfill, so to speak. When the soul moves on from this life, it sheds the body and the egoic self, the two densest aspects we have on Earth. The body is physical and the ego is energetic; negative-based energy, to be exact. Because its vibration is low, the ego cannot go where the soul goes in the afterlife. Where a person passes is where the "ego shadow" is left.

These shadow people can move, form attachments, and follow people who interact with them because they feed off energy, especially fear. This is why many of these investigators experience things being thrown at them or hear dark, brooding voices during investigations. If I could pass on one piece of advice to anyone conducting paranormal investigations, it would be this: Go into a space with a high vibrational frequency and maintain it through wakeful meditation while in that particular space. Doing so will be protective and help prevent these shadow people from attaching themselves, averting having to deal with the consequences later on.

Negative Experiences Serve a Purpose

Let's take a look at how paranormal phenomena and psychic abilities serve a purpose, a soul purpose. Let's start with psychic abilities. The fact that you've experienced moments of intuition should tell you that there's more to life than what the five senses can perceive. I also feel that having even one extrasensory perception experience speaks volumes on so many levels. An ESP event informs and enlightens the one who is having the experience. It's a way of the universe telling you there is more to life than the physical and material; in fact, it's all a matter of spirit.

Paranormal phenomena can also open one's eyes to another world. And depending on your readiness to make the shift to sixth chakra consciousness, it can be the final catalyst to catapult you forward. I'll make this brief and to the point because I already mentioned my 2005 evening with a night terror in the introduction. That particular experience was so transforming because it was the first time in my life where I really felt helpless. I did not understand what was happening in my bedroom that night, nor did I know its purpose. I was dealing with something dark and paranormal and didn't know how to protect myself. But what seemed like such a horrible and undesirable experience really ended up being a gift; it created a white-hot desire within me to understand. Fueled by desire and a profound willingness to know, I received what I asked for weeks later: clarity, wisdom, and understanding through third eye activation. What seemed to be such a terrifying experience actually served a purpose: it led me to the awareness and reality of my soul.

What I want to point out from this example is that a negative experience (or an undesired experience, for that matter) is one way the universe communicates with you. These experiences speak to you, telling you that your current level of consciousness is no longer serving you and that in order to transcend these undesirable experiences, you're going to have to make a shift. It's a change in awareness from separation to oneness; from uncertainty, fear, and doubt to the safety, certainty, and understanding of your highest self.

A Curious Apparition

Being empathetic, I understand the emotions and intense energies felt by those who are energetically sensitive. Empaths just feel more; they experience the emotions of others around them. It is important for empaths to maintain a high vibrational frequency through inner stillness to protect themselves from the bombardment of lower energies. There are also empaths who can see more through hyperawareness.

Let me start by saying that had I not been so energetically aware of my surroundings, I would have never witnessed what I am about to share with you. In the fall of 2008, I was living in a semi-detached house right across the street from a cemetery. I had lived there for a year or so before I began to experience anything paranormal. One afternoon, I decided to visit my local bookstore. I grabbed my car keys and headed out the door. As I opened the front door to exit my house, intuition grabbed my attention and I was guided to look to my right. There, at four o'clock in the afternoon, a female apparition dressed in black looked intently into my neighbor's window. The house was raised and from what I can remember, the bottom of the window was at least five feet off the ground. Her head and shoulders were about two feet above the window ledge. By my estimate, she was over six feet tall.

This experience lasted only a few seconds, but I remember many details. The bottom of her dress was in motion and flowing, like it was wisping in the wind. After a second or two, she turned around and looked at me with anger and shock; her eyes opened so much that I could see the whites of her eyes. Then, right in front of me, she began to become a circle of energy, becoming smaller and smaller until she vanished entirely. I stood there frozen for a few more moments, trying to come to terms with what I just saw.

Following that experience, I decided to keep my blinds closed for as long as I lived there, which was for another few years. I did not do this out of fear; the idea of something or someone from beyond this world peeking into my window just didn't sit well with me. I later came to realize that the area was a hub, a portal for paranormal phenomena, as I had other paranormal experiences while I lived there.

Being incredibly sensitive or hyperaware can have its pluses and … I don't really want to call them minuses, but you get my drift. With hyperawareness and developed psychic abilities, you're going to have experiences; some will be mystical and some will be paranormal. But really, it's only paranormal when viewed from the perspective of your five senses. Through sixth chakra consciousness, it's just the spirit world and all the expressions of consciousness found within it.

Dealing with Darker Energies

Living in that home across from the cemetery was a course in the subtle and not-so-subtle nature of the paranormal. I experienced an array of phenomena, some of which were quite negative. Because your heightened awareness will allow you to perceive these energies with greater discernment, I felt it quite important to offer some guidance for how to approach and deal with these experiences if they happen. Looking back, I see the purpose in those experiences: I need to share them and shed light on paranormal phenomena so that fear can be dispelled.

The first thing I want to make clear is that any paranormal experience should be approached with understanding and fearlessness. Some experiences are benign, but they can be startling nevertheless. For example, one evening while I sat on the couch watching one of my favorite ghost-hunting shows (of all things), I observed a tall, slender shadow person walk from my kitchen area across my family room and through my entertainment unit, walking briskly into the adjacent home. It seemed to walk past me with little or no awareness of me sitting just a few feet away.

I sat there for a moment, contemplating what I just saw. I got up and played with the lighting, trying to determine if it could have been a flickering light even though I knew the lights hadn't changed during the experience. I could not re-create what I had witnessed, so I just accepted what had transpired. That was the first and only time I experienced a shadow person in that home.

This next paranormal experience could be viewed as terrifying to some, but with understanding of what one is dealing with and with a fearless spirit, one is empowered and able to dispatch anything through the power of unconditional love.

I've always been a light sleeper, but this particular night I was more awake than anything else. It was around 3:30 a.m. I was resting on the couch when I began to hear something like the chattering of teeth; that's the best description I have for the sound. (Keep in mind that this is about two years post–chakra activation so I was prepared for anything, unlike the time I experienced a negative entity two years earlier.) As I turned to see where the noise was coming from, I was briefly alarmed by what I saw. Three dark hooded figures, walking one behind the other, were slowly walking toward me. I could not see their faces. Their gait was somewhat erratic, shifting side to side as they approached. They couldn't have been more than five feet tall.

My first response was to take a pillow and swing it at them. I swung and watched as the pillow went right through them, accomplishing nothing. That's when I stood up, feeling the presence of unconditional love rise up in me, and walked directly at them. As I met them, I witnessed them dissolve in the presence of my centered and unmoved consciousness. They simply vanished right in front of me.

Reflecting back on this experience, wisdom tells me it would have been a different experience had I reacted rather than responded. These negative entities need to feed off of fear; they need a reaction, but found none in me. Had I become terrified, they would have tormented me and would have continued to do so as long as I lived there. Instead, I knew the area was a hub for paranormal phenomena, but more importantly, I knew what these entities were relative to who and what I am: they were illusions, fear manifested, attempting to feed off energy.

The last experience I had in this home occurred about six months prior to my moving. It was about 6:00 a.m. and I was fairly awake when I heard a loud, audible growl. It was deep and guttural, the kind a tiger would make. My eyes widened and I sprung out of bed to make sure some animal hadn't gotten into the house, but of course, there was nothing. It was another attempt to frighten me, perhaps to force me out so that someone else could move in who might be a more favorable, reactive target.

On my last day in that house, I was guided to do a spiritual banishing and protective exercise. This was something I had never done before, but I felt it was quite effective. "I banish you from this house," I repeated a few times as I walked through it. "You are not permitted to follow me." It's important to note that these statements were said through an awareness of authority, power, strength, and fearlessness. In other words, there wasn't an ounce of doubt within me as I spoke. As I finished the exercise, I could feel a change in the atmosphere of the house. It felt lighter. I left a final blessing on the home as I walked out the door for the last time.

You can hopefully see what a difference it makes to approach paranormal phenomena consciously. It shifts the power from the entity to the one witnessing it. These darker energies want a reaction because that opens you up to attachment so they can continue to feed off of your energy. The way to deal with them is by claiming your power and realizing that Source is with you always. The light of consciousness within you is the only real power there is; it can cast out any fear, anything unlike itself. With all this being said, I felt that an exercise and some pointers in self-protection from darker entities would be appropriate.

Paranormal Protection Protocol

When you operate from greater awareness through an activated third eye, you're going to be able to perceive entities from time to time. You may even come to experience a paranormal event or two. There is nothing to fear when you approach these experiences with understanding and a spirit of fearlessness. The following protocol is how to protect yourself if such an encounter should occur.

If you should witness a shadow figure or apparition or if you hear something out of the ordinary, do the following:

1. First, remember that when you are centered in the present moment and when you are mindful and aware of the power of your inner being, no entity or dark shadow can withstand that power. The power of your inner being is an immoveable force based in the all-consuming power of unconditional love. In other words, know that love is much, much more powerful than any fear.

2. Do not engage the entity by asking, "Who are you?" This is what they want; they want to draw you in to create a potential attachment.

3. Rather, observe and respond if necessary. Give the entity no reaction, but rather be still and centered in your power. Reaction is what opens the door to fear, and fear is what they feed on.

4. If you feel threatened and must respond, say and do the following: If you are inside your home, open a window or door and say with authority, "I command you to leave this space immediately," "I cast you out now," or "I call upon Archangel Michael to come to my aide now." Michael is a powerful archangel who protects and assists us when called upon.

5. Keep in mind that whenever I've encountered these entities in an outside environment, my awareness of them and
my centeredness was enough to send them packing. They
are aware of who is and isn't afraid of them, so be fearless
in their presence. Let nothing move you and know who is
with you at all times: Source, the all-encompassing one.

Everything Is Information

When you operate from higher awareness, every person you meet
and every experience, paranormal or otherwise, can serve you as
a gift in contrast, a lesson to remember or some gem of insight
that you otherwise would not have received. Everything serves a
purpose because within everything, seen and unseen, is information. Being aware enough to recognize, read, and decipher that
information is what makes the difference. The universe is always
speaking to you.

When you look at a clock, it gives you information, the time.
If you walk across the street without looking both ways and suddenly hear a car honk, the driver is informing you to get out of the
way. When you attend a workshop, you gain specific information
on a particular subject. When you have a conversation with your
partner or spouse, you receive information about how they feel.
Everything is information. Information comes through a variety
of ways through the five senses, but it also operates through the
sixth chakra on an energetic and vibratory level.

The goal is to integrate the two in order to allow the whole
of you to operate as one so that all information can be received
clearly. This involves "feeling" the information by looking at the
deeper meaning of it. Just to be clear, I'm not talking about over-
analyzing a conversation, but rather allowing the truth behind it

to reveal itself through greater spiritual awareness. Effort is not required; allow intuition to be expressed and recognized. You don't have to try, you just *are* that intuition, that awareness, that clarity. Allow the energy behind it all to speak to you. Pay attention. Information beyond what the five senses can perceive is always being offered to you.

For example, let's say you had a conversation with someone a few days ago but left it somewhat confused. You can go back and meditate upon the conversation and allow clarity to express itself with some simple attention to what was said. Allow the energy of the conversation to speak to you clearly by keeping the ego's perception of it out of the way. In other words, suspend all judgment. Information always comes when one is relaxed and not trying to extract something, but rather allowing it to be received; this is what is called retrocognition. Retrocognition is being able to obtain knowledge that wasn't available at the time from a past event.

The insight is in allowing, not trying. Looking at something without effort; placing attention without straining. Clarity always comes when invited, not forced. It's a softer approach that is also incredibly powerful at the same time.

Having increased sensitivity to the energies around you makes you more perceptive and leads you to the truth of the matter. It makes you question what you're feeling so that you're not simply dismissing your feelings, but honoring them by listening to them consciously and allowing information to speak to you. I want to end this section with a paranormal experience I recently had while house hunting. It's a fitting demonstration of how an activated sixth chakra and heightened awareness can be of service, giving you the clarity and ability to read many different types of energy, including the paranormal variety.

Wanting a little bit more room, I decided I was going to move out of my townhouse and purchase a detached home. I found a house on a real estate website and contacted the realtor whose name was on the listing. After asking a few initial questions over the phone, we agreed to meet the following afternoon.

I had some initial excitement about the house because it seemed to check off a lot of things I wanted in a home and it looked like it was located in a nice neighborhood. The morning came and I made the two-hour trek to see the house. I brought a measuring tape to check room sizes and a receptacle tester to check the electrical outlets in the house to make sure they were working properly. I usually have a home inspector look at the electrical work, but I had decided not to due to timing. When I met the realtor, she said she would unlock the house and wait for me in the backyard; she was going to give me time to inspect the home.

When I first walked into the home, I sensed a slight heaviness in the air but I quickly dismissed it. The living room was located to the left immediately upon entry, and I decided to start there. The living room seemed to be fine in terms of size and from an electrical standpoint. And from an energetic standpoint, the space also felt fairly clear. Behind the living room was the first bedroom. That's where things got a little interesting. I entered the bedroom only to be immediately hit with feelings of sadness, dread, fear, and even the feeling of death. I also noticed that even though I had turned on both lights in the bedroom, it still seemed dark.

I liked the house so much that I tried to ignore what I was sensing and continued inspecting the rest of the house. The energy in the rest of the house seemed clear as opposed to the first bedroom.

After finishing the house inspection, I went to the backyard and toured the garage. As I entered, I felt as if I was intruding on the space. I felt somewhat unwelcome. I walked back outside and felt guided to go back to the first bedroom. The agent followed me back in and waited for me in the hallway.

Back in the bedroom, those initial feelings I had were now intensified. I couldn't imagine myself staying in that room for another five minutes, let alone sleeping there. Finally, I called out to the realtor and said, "I have to ask you a question. Did someone pass away in this house, in this room?"

The realtor remained silent for a moment, and I sensed her surprise even though she remained in the hallway, out of sight. "Yes, an elderly couple just passed away in there a few weeks apart from each other, just recently."

I was initially taken aback by her affirmation. This was the first time I had encountered such intense energy. I said a prayer for the couple before exiting the room and met the realtor near the front door. She looked amazed that I had picked up on that. We chatted for another few minutes and then I told her this wasn't the house for me.

I decided not to purchase for a few reasons. For one thing, there was an ongoing issue with the backyard's property line that could result in losing several feet of property, according to the realtor. And from a spiritual awareness standpoint, the intensity in the bedroom was quite overwhelming. Although I know I could have eventually cleared that space, my gut feeling was not to proceed with the purchase. I also felt that the attachment was so incredibly strong that some form of energy would always remain in the room. Though it wasn't necessarily harmful energy, I knew I needed to follow my intuition.

This was an unexpected paranormal encounter with many lessons. It reminded me to read my surroundings and not to dismiss my feelings or inner guidance system. It also helped me use the eye of clarity to see what was before me. It gave me a clear understanding of contrasting energies and heightened my awareness even further. From my point of view, this experience wasn't a waste of time whatsoever; it was a gift in greater understanding.

chapter twelve
THIRD EYE MANAGEMENT

If you've made it this far, you have the desire to open your third eye and you have opened yourself up to activating it. You may have had some insights and experienced some moments of heightened awareness, or perhaps even a paranormal experience. But in talking about increasing your sensitivity to energy and the spirit world around you, we also have to discuss how to manage these abilities and protect yourself. Here's the thing: if you're just beginning to experience heightened awareness through a blossoming third eye, there can be times when such heightened awareness may be sensory overload or you may find that you're just not ready or willing to always feel the spirit world around you. For example, if mediumship is one of your strengths, you'll want to know how to close off communication from the other side so that you don't become too overwhelmed. We'll address that later in this chapter.

Keep in mind that we exist and operate within an infinitely intelligent universe, and you're not going to be given levels of awareness that you're not ready to receive. Don't worry about not being ready for these spiritual gifts—you already have them; third eye activation only heightens them. It is also important not to approach the process of activating this chakra with fear or trepidation because, as I mentioned earlier, we are working with the universal law of cause and effect. In other words, like attracts like. But with that being said, we all have personal preferences, and there may be times when you want to close yourself off to your abilities and just experience being human. This is called balance or human-spirit integration.

Protective Techniques

The third eye operates automatically, usually without one's conscious awareness. It's for this reason that most people dismiss their psychic events or intuitive experiences as hunches or gut feelings. But through intention and greater awareness, its potential can be increased and activated more fully, making us more sensitive energetically. With that being said, there are things we can do to reduce that sensitivity, thereby protecting ourselves from experiencing too much psychic energy or paranormal phenomena. Let's now look at some simple methods to help manage third eye awareness.

• Third Eye Management
• Visualization Technique •

All experience starts with intention, and the intention here is to communicate to your highest self that you want to reduce your awareness to the energy around you. This technique is so simple that it only takes a minute or two to accomplish the desired result. Again, exertion or effort is not required; simply use focused imagery.

1. Find a quiet space where you can sit comfortably. Close your eyes and take a few deep breaths. Relax your shoulders.

2. Imagine the third eye as an actual eye in the middle of your forehead. Visualize it gently closing. As you see it closing in your mind, give thanks for the reduction in energy information being offered. (This imagery doesn't actually close the third eye, as it is an automatic spiritual faculty, but it signals to your highest self to reduce your sensitivity to its power of awareness. In other words, intention creates reality.)

3. After visualizing the third eye closing for five or ten seconds, take a deep breath. Then let the experience and moment go.

Use this exercise as needed. It is especially helpful if you're experiencing an excess of extrasensory perception.

• Spoken Intentions Exercise •

This is another simple but quite effective exercise. Using the spoken word sets the tone for reducing energy information or paranormal phenomena. When speaking your intentions, do so with confidence. Know that what you're speaking will come to pass. Do not doubt the power of your intention.

These intentions only need to be uttered when you feel it necessary, and they should be said when you have a minute or two to yourself:

1. **"I am surrounded by the light and love of Source Energy."** This is a powerful and protective intention because there is no darkness that can penetrate the power and vibrational frequency of light and love. Fear, which is what negative entities feed off of, cannot tolerate unconditional love; its frequency is all-consuming. By acknowledging Source Energy and embracing the safety of The All That Is, you create a cocoon of protection.

2. **"No harm can come to me. I am unharmable."** This is a very effective and incredibly protective intention. Speaking this affirmation activates spiritual support around you.

3. **"I am closing the door to anything not of peace, wisdom, and clarity."** Energetically speaking, this intention sets the stage for only your spirit guides and other high-vibrating beings to come in contact with you. Words are powerful, even more so than thoughts. Uttering this phrase sends out a high and powerful vibrational frequency all around you.

4. **"Thank you for protecting me tonight and every night."** Combining gratitude with spiritual protection, this intention should be spoken every evening just before bed. Negative entities like to appear late at night, usually when we are drifting off to sleep or while we are sleeping because we appear more vulnerable to them. Speaking this intention raises your vibrational frequency because you know that you are being protected. Put faith in your intentions.

5. **"My third eye is balanced."** Having too much of anything can create imbalance. By sending this intention into the universe, it goes out and returns to you, thereby aligning you with the intention itself. As you are aligned with the intention, you will create that inner balance on a conscious

level, either through meditation or affirmations, which can then be reflected outwardly.

6. **"My awareness is protected."** Short and to the point, this intention invokes the power of consciousness to shield your conscious awareness when you are in crowds or gatherings. Energy vampires are people who unconsciously thrive on drama, and affirming this phrase raises energetic walls around you that make it difficult for lower-vibrating energies to feed off your life force.

Be Human

This section is about grounding yourself in your humanness to bring your awareness back to this third-dimensional reality, or the manifested world around you. It's all about having balance. Integrated spirituality is when you have one hand on the ground while the other reaches for higher consciousness. Having this balanced awareness helps prevent chakra imbalance by merging the energy of this reality with higher consciousness.

Bringing your focus back to the manifested world shifts your perception, giving you a break from the spiritual world around you. You may choose to do this whenever you feel sensory overload from elevated awareness or when you feel that your spiritual aspect needs to be balanced with your human aspect. Some telltale signs that you need to ground yourself into your humanity are: you feel like you can't relate to others as easily as before; you're wanting to isolate yourself more and more because your elevated awareness isn't meshing with others; and you're letting things that were once important to you fall to the wayside because of your spiritual life.

Grounding your energy will bring balance to your expanded awareness.

Ten Ways to Ground Your Energy

1. **Spend time with friends or family.** We live in a world of contrast. Everyone is operating at different levels of awareness, and that's perfectly fine. Spending time with loved ones reminds you of the gift in contrast and allows you to engage your personality, your sense of humor, and other aspects of your humanness.

2. **Go to a movie, show, or concert.** Living the spiritual life doesn't mean you have to sacrifice the things you enjoy doing. And being human does not for one moment diminish your spirituality, so get out and enjoy!

3. **Move your body.** The physical body was designed to be used, and that includes physical exercise. Engage your physicality and hit the gym or go for a walk.

4. **Take a trip.** Whether it's a day trip or a weeklong vacation, exploring brings your focus to this world, which reminds you of the beauty that can be found within it.

5. **Volunteer your time.** Spending time being of service to others can be a reminder that all of us, in some way, are dealing with adversity. That grounds you in compassion.

6. **Make a phone call.** Technology is wonderful, but sometimes it can get in the way of how we relate to each other. It can become a roadblock to real human interaction, like speaking to one another.

7. **Write a letter of appreciation to someone.** Reflecting on another's kindness toward you is a wonderful reminder

that deep down, we are all the same. By expressing your gratitude to someone you appreciate, you open your heart chakra and remember your humanity in the process.

8. **Use affirmations.** "I am grounded in the earth while being aware of who I am" and "I am a spiritual being having a human experience, and I honor my humanity" are two great affirmations that shift things on an energetic level and remind you that you are one with Earth.

9. **Take a look at some old photos.** Looking at who you once were and then reflecting on how far you've come not only gives you greater perspective, it gives you an appreciation for any adversity you've had along the way. It helps you realize that every challenge led you to greater awareness and personal growth.

10. **Remember why you're here.** Yes, we each have a soul purpose on Earth, and that is to remember who we are spiritually. But remember, this would not be possible without our human aspect, which brings the highs and lows, the challenges and triumphs.

Setting Boundaries

If you are called into mediumship, it is important to know how to close the door to the other side and how to set boundaries. When you have this gift, those on the other side know it and will understandably try to get your attention when you're in the vicinity of one of their loved ones who are still living here on Earth. Not being able to say no to these spiritual beings can become exhausting.

Here are a few things you can say or do to manage spirit interaction.

Managing Spirit Interaction

- Say **"I am closed to spirit communication today"** or **"My energy field is shielded today."** Choose not to focus on anyone else's energy as you interact with them, but focus only on yourself. In other words, center your awareness on you and only you. You're allowed to be self-centered once in a while. By doing this, you reduce the amount of energetic information you receive.

- **Have a conversation with your spirit guides.** Letting them know when and how you are available can keep you from being spiritually bombarded. Letting them know that you don't want any evening or night communication, for example, can curtail or even totally prevent being visited in your dreams.

- **Imagine a wall of energy or a circle of white light surrounding you before you head out for the day.** This sends the message "Sorry, not today," to the other side. It makes it clear that you are not open to communicating and engaging. Remember that everything is energy, and creating that wall or circle of white light in your mind really creates it on a spiritual level.

- **Choose to not engage.** Spirit communicates through feelings and images. By simply observing the communication and choosing not to respond, you are signaling to the spirit that communication is not going to take place. In other words, nonengagement closes the door to discussion. It's not the warmest approach, but is sometimes called for to maintain your own energetic inner balance.

Final Thoughts

As you embark on this journey to unlocking and mastering your psychic abilities, there are some final thoughts I want to share with you.

Remember that what you become aware of and focus on is what is realized in your experience.

These extraordinary abilities cannot be added to you; they can only be remembered and allowed to express themselves, as they are a part of consciousness itself.

Be patient with yourself; try less and allow more.

The sixth chakra is an incredible gift with profound potential to elevate virtually every area of your life. There is a version of you already fully engaging it in the quantum field. I am reminding you of this because I want to further stir up the desire within you. The desire and intensity to know, understand, and express the clarity that manifests these psychic treasures is the soul's very own desire. After all, this is what we're all here for: to fulfill our life's purpose and become the greatest version of ourselves.

appendix

QUESTIONS AND ANSWERS

Every piece of information and every exercise offered in this book came with a single purpose: to assist you in taking the next step toward opening the third eye so you can unlock your limitless potential and master your psychic abilities. Clarity, wisdom, understanding, awareness, inner peace, stillness, the paranormal, your psychic abilities ... all of these elements are intertwined. They are all expressed and experienced fully through one spiritual faculty: an activated sixth chakra. Using questions and answers, I will offer more insight and guidance to help you move closer to the intended goal.

Some of these questions have come from workshops I have held; others have manifested spontaneously by tapping in to other minds seeking further clarification. Some I have called forth by asking the highest self or Source Energy for further clarification on a particular area. Be mindful that when you ask a question, answers are received.

Q: How do I know if I am progressing toward activating the third eye?
A: There are a few telltale signs. You may begin to experience some increased emotional turbulence. As your awareness increases overall, so will your awareness of emotions like deep fear. These moments of hyperawareness should not be alarming; welcome them. You are moving toward higher awareness and higher dimensions of consciousness.

As you elevate, you may find yourself becoming a voracious spiritual reader interested in different points of view. Your desire for the experience of inner stillness will increase, and you'll find yourself entering a space of meditation more and more frequently. This desire is preparing you for the quantum leap into sixth chakra consciousness, which is the frequency of perfect clarity.

Q: Can we talk some more about clearing energy blockages?
A: The key here is being aware of them and then identifying the emotions behind them. Energy blockages will all be ultimately based in some version of fear that can easily be masked as doubt, frustration, the fear of loss, or anger. Avoiding these emotions will keep one stuck, so it's important to face them; it's part of the process to becoming spiritually mature. Looking at these emotional blockages through awareness is usually enough to cause them to disperse. If you starve fear through observation and nonreaction, you will automatically nourish the soul. Remember that fear is only as powerful as you believe it to be. Revoke its power and reclaim yours.

Be mindful of the power of forgiveness; it is the key to releasing yourself and others. Forgiveness is a literal force that has the potential and power to cast out long-standing negative emotions or blocks. It's that powerful.

Q: It seems that the activation of the third eye and enlightenment go hand in hand. Can you elaborate on this?
A: An activating third eye is your spiritual awakening event. Clarity takes place in literally the blink of an eye. Human conditioning is transcended, leaving one free of negativity and the burdens of emotion; you become emotionally light. You *become* the light through inner awakening. And through an activated third eye, the channel for perfect clarity is fully opened, allowing universal intelligence to pour wisdom and understanding into you once you've been emptied of the ego. It's not that wisdom and understanding weren't always being offered, they were, it's just that they weren't recognized as such due to the incessantness of the ego.

Q: What are some other practices that I can employ to help raise my vibrational frequency?
A: There are many things you can do while you are on the path to becoming. For example, go out for a leisurely drive and listen to your favorite music. Pay close attention to what's going on in the mind during activities like this. Your awareness is focused on what is before you, the drive or the melodies, which tends to cause temporary ego transcendence without the individual really being aware of it. This is quite an effective practice: become aware and allow awareness to fill your consciousness.

Q: What is ego death and how does it relate to this chakra?
A: Ego death is the end of the ego's control over your consciousness; it loses its power over you. In other words, unconditional love is embraced as reality and fear is released because it's seen as an illusion relative to the truth within you. When the sixth chakra is activated, it is the beginning of the end for the false self and all of its trappings. You will still experience the ego post–chakra activation, but it will shift from being a source of pain to one of contrast. Through ego death, you will realize that there is no power whatsoever in illusions; therein lies your freedom.

Q: Can you further describe inner stillness?
A: Before enlightenment, it's in the background of your awareness, virtually unnoticeable due to the incessant stream of thought provided by the ego. If you looked closely at your stream of thinking, you would notice the pauses, the nothingness in between your thoughts—that is stillness. It is the essence of your inner being and the channel for inner peace, clarity, and wisdom. Third eye activation is an undoing of the ego, allowing your inner being and inner stillness to come to the forefront of your consciousness. This turn of events leaves one with a still mind, a mind of peace and clarity, which is the perfect channel for divine wisdom and guidance.

Q: How vital is it to challenge negative thinking?
A: It's quite important on a few levels. Challenging negative thoughts weakens the ego while opening up the channel of the sixth chakra. The more you put this into practice, the more automatic it will become. The more automatic it becomes, the greater the discernment you will experience. With greater clarity, you will know when you're being faced with negativity. Challenging negative thinking also neutralizes the emotions tied to them.

This emotional neutralization, in turn, raises your vibrational frequency, allowing for greater intuition and several spiritual faculties to begin to be realized.

Q: Why did we have to "forget" our spiritual nature?
A: Forgetfulness is necessary because if you were told that you were already in the kingdom and one with Source Energy, you would lack a point of reference. There would be nothing to compare it to. Forgetfulness allows for the full experience of who and what you are by experiencing the ego, which is all that you're not.

Q: Is it accurate to say that our psychic abilities are simply extensions of who we really are?
A: That would be a very accurate statement. You have supernatural spiritual abilities that are beyond the five senses. They are based in energy, vibration, and information. The greater your clarity, the more information you can become aware of. This allows you to experience a fuller, richer, and more empowered life.

Q: Awareness was really emphasized in this book. Is there anything else that should be mentioned about it?
A: Awareness gives life to what you focus on. Your focused awareness on your ego is what made it your reality. But, a shift in focus—your focused awareness on inner stillness—can also be made your reality as you consciously release or forget the egoic mind. Furthermore, awareness gives you the option to choose differently. It is heightened alertness, allowing you to observe and be present with regard to your own consciousness.

Q: The reality of Source Energy really seems to be beyond any human comprehension. How much more understanding of Source is possible through sixth chakra consciousness?

A: Through sixth chakra activation you come to understand through direct experience the one true nature of Source Energy, which is unconditional love. The experience not only solidifies your faith but allows you to completely trust Source and the process.

Words are limited in describing the limitless that is Source, but a glimpse is given to the power of Source Energy through the realization that all events, past and present, are happening in this moment. That power is further witnessed by recognizing the same essence in all things, all people, and all the nothingness around us. Through the awakened state, Source is remembered as a friend, a guide, a loving parent, a redeemer, a deliverer, a great helper in time of need, and an unfailing partner who makes all things possible.

Q: Can you talk a little more about the subtle body and energy medicine? How does raising your vibrational frequency lead to a potential physical healing?

A: The subtle body is an extension of the highest self, and when the energy of this body is allowed to flow freely, inner harmony is achieved and translated as health. When that energy is blocked by fear via one's ego, disruption of cellular activity occurs. This inner conflict, if allowed to continue year after year, can possibly be transferred to the physical body.

Energy medicine or energy healing is essentially any modality that allows the release of negative emotions that are affecting the subtle body's energy wheels, chakras. For example, energetic or emotional healing can be achieved through meditation, visualization, or challenging negative thinking. Raising your vibrational frequency by meditating on inner stillness moves the conditioned mind out of the way, inviting infinite intelligence's unconditional love to flow freely, which in turn allows for a vibrational shift.

Q: It seems that the more spiritually aware one is, the more encounters one has with the paranormal. Why is that?

A: It's not so much that you'll come to experience more paranormal phenomena, but because of your hyperawareness through the awakened state, you will be that much more in tune with subtle and not-so-subtle energies and "things that go bump in the night." Where you once were distracted by the egoic mind, clarity now reveals what is around you visually and energetically. Spiritual sonar, for example, intentionally sends out waves of energy, and the waves return to you with information. But even when you're not applying spiritual sonar consciously, your attunement to your environment through oneness will always provide energetic feedback.

Q: What would you say is one of the most transformative exercises you can employ to make the shift to sixth chakra consciousness?

A: The practice of silent meditation; the meditation upon inner stillness. There is no "higher form" of meditation, nor is there a higher form of prayer, than this. This form of meditation is direct communication with the soul via the channel of the sixth chakra. Inner stillness is sixth chakra consciousness and it's the frequency of the universe. All wisdom, divine guidance, and intuition are delivered through this channel. It is pure in frequency and perfectly clear.

Q: Can you describe how single vision is experienced?
A: Single vision is experienced through a silent mind, through the pure awareness of consciousness. This vision goes beyond appearances while the silent witness or inner being within you looks out at the world. Through this clear, singular vision, the ego is silenced and your environment is seen through inner stillness and the reality of oneness. In other words, everything and everyone is seen as one, despite appearances.

Q: Are we sharing this world with other interdimensional beings?
A: Let me start by saying that there are no limits to consciousness, or to creation for that matter. Are there other, more highly evolved beings coming in and out of this world and dimension? Yes, absolutely. There is a lot more going on in the "nothingness" than one can imagine.

Portals can be opened or created using thought. Many of you understand this already and create portals whenever you decide to use a spirit board. There is often fear and a lack of understanding when it comes to energy, and you attract the same energy that you are already operating with. Unfortunately, that is why so many people end up calling forth darker entities. Raise your vibrational frequency and you'll find that not only will a spirit board not be necessary, but you will choose to only call upon beings of light, ascended masters, or spirit guides.

Q: Are there any limits to what one can evolve to become?
A: Enlightenment is only the beginning. Evolution is a never-ending process. No limits have been laid upon you, nor will they ever. Can you imagine evolving to become exactly like Source Energy? You already are. But you have much to release and let go of in terms of your human conditioning. When this is accomplished,

you will receive a glimpse of your potential, and it's awe-inspiring to say the least. Are you beginning to understand what kind of power you are one with and operating through on a moment-by-moment basis?

Q: It sounds like there are alternate dimensions that can be accessed. Is this possible?
A: There is infinitely more to consciousness than can ever be said or written. There are infinite versions of yourself, and any one of these versions or realities can be called forth through unconscious or conscious choosing. There is a version of you that is a self-realizing enlightened being. There is a version of you that remains stuck. There is a version of you on the road to enlightenment. Intention, direction of thought, and focus are what allow access to a more desirable alternate reality. Your thoughts are doorways to alternate dimensions of experience. These realities largely go unnoticed because of human conditioning, but the more aware you become, the more aware you can become of becoming.

Q: What is personal mastery?
A: It's a shift in consciousness and a shift in perception. Mastery is the conquering of the ego through the practice of nonreaction. It is a moment-by-moment way of living through your authentic, still self. It doesn't require effort, but it does call for release of the emotions that attempt to control you. A hyperaware state of being, it is both a relaxed and alert state at the same time. At this level of awareness, one is no longer led by emotions but is instead guided by infinite intelligence through the channel of the sixth chakra.

Q: How does forgiveness tie in with clarity and the honing of your psychic abilities?

A: Forgiveness is a powerful and all-encompassing force. It is what undoes the past, releasing you and your consciousness from emotional bondage. Forgiveness lightens your energetic field, allowing for greater clarity and intuition in the process. It is the slate cleaner for your past. By forgiving yourself, others, and even Source if necessary, your past is let go, which allows a more empowered present and a brighter future.

Q: Some would say that psychic abilities come from another source—that they are not from Source Energy. What are your thoughts on this?

A: Your psychic abilities are a part of you, and they can't be added to you or taken away. As for the source of them, they certainly aren't extensions of the ego. The ego is darkness and confusion. Intuition, clairvoyance, and telepathy are extensions of your inner being. When clarity is amplified, awareness of these gifts also increases. There is nothing "wrong" whatsoever with having these gifts because this is how communication is accomplished in the spiritual realm, a realm in which you're already in.

Q: Can you further elaborate on how an activated third eye activates all the other chakras?

A: The third eye is the energy commander; it is what is responsible for clarity and for clearing all negative emotion. Once activated, it opens the channel to the seventh chakra, which is our connection to universal intelligence. This allows the flow of universal energy to reach and activate the other chakras freely. An automatic energy balancer, the sixth chakra clears the way for an energetic shift, causing a high-vibrational frequency to be experienced throughout your entire being.

Q: It seems that relaxation is helpful for accessing psychic abilities. Is this true?

A: Yes, the more relaxed one is, the easier it becomes to discern subtle energies and information from higher dimensions of consciousness. And nothing can help you achieve great relaxation more than the practice of meditation.

Q: If the spiritual world is here and now, does that mean that matter is spirit in form?

A: Everything manifested and unmanifested is an expression of Source Energy. Everything and everyone is made up of the same stuff; the only difference is how that stuff is arranged. One arrangement of universal energy results in a plant, a different arrangement in a mountain, and another arrangement results in a human being. If you go beyond appearances and enter the quantum state, everything is made up of the same energy, the same nothingness. This is why you can't be angry at a person, place, or thing without experiencing that anger yourself, because all is one.

Q: Are all your fears transcended with sixth chakra activation?

A: All your fears are released, including the one that weighs on the minds of many: the fear of death. In the awakened state, death is seen as transformation. Living moment by moment, the master allows the last moment to pass in order to be reborn in the next. As you continue to evolve and spiritually grow, there may be some residual fears that attempt to hold you back, but even these will prove to be catalysts for further growth. Think of an elastic band—the farther you pull it back, the farther it will travel when released.

Q: Can you offer a few more tips for automatic writing?
A: One should be relaxed and in a state of allowing. Focus on a topic and give in to the energy within you. Allow yourself to be guided. Try not to think of what is going to be written, but go beyond the ego and permit the soul to express its innate wisdom. When you feel inspired, act on it.

Q: Please talk a little bit more about silent/active listening. How is this achieved?
A: Be present in your mind, body, and soul. Let your awareness become one with intuition. Allow yourself to become one with spiritual guidance. Drop all self-created egoic walls and get to the heart of the matter, which is the stillness within. Focus on that and live from the inside out, not the outside in. In other words, place your attention on the greater awareness within you.

Q: What happens after enlightenment?
A: What do you desire to have happen? You will continue to evolve and you will be called to be of service in some way. Your passions don't die after your spiritual awakening. You can still have a life while being life itself. If you are a police officer pre-activation, you can still remain one following awakening, but will you want to? You can be both an incredible chef and a self-actualized person. Why not? You are free to choose. You can be, do, and have anything. So choose, become, take action, allow, trust, and experience. You are the CEO of your life.

Q: Would it be accurate to say that stress is a roadblock to accessing psychic abilities?

A: Stress only serves a purpose until it no longer does. It can be a catalyst to a spontaneous awakening, but it can also be a hindrance. Chronic stress can prevent you from being able to read and discern spiritually guided information because of its lower-vibrating energy. In a nutshell, stress is accumulated negative energy in the form of resistance, the past, and/or the future. The key to releasing stress is becoming one with the now.

Q: Are we living in an information-based universe?

A: Yes, but let's expand on this. Everything is information and communication. Universal energy is being offered through intuition, vibrations, feelings, and countless other ways so you can receive the intended message. The message could be on the next billboard you see, in a book, or in a fortune cookie. The universe will employ whatever is required; that even includes experience. Think about it—there are messages and information in all of your circumstances, whether they are desirable or undesirable. So pay attention. Source is always communicating with you in many, many ways.

Q: Would it be accurate to say that there is potential in everything?

A: Absolutely, because Source Energy is in everything. Change can come in an instant. Where you have started does not have to be where you end. Look around you; look what has been created from nothing. All things are possible. Source created your physical body and its infinite intelligence remains with you, within you, as you. It's not a question if Source Energy is ready; the question is, are you ready? Are you ready to make the shift, activate the sixth chakra, and become all that you could potentially become?

Q: If just three things had to be taken away from this book to create an atmosphere for chakra activation, what would they be?
A:

1. Practice living in the now.

2. Challenge your automatic negative thoughts.

3. Cultivate awareness. There is a lot more available to you than just the five senses.

Q: Is the ego the only thing standing in the way of sixth chakra consciousness and the mastery of psychic abilities?
A: Yes, but there's more to it. The ego is an idea of separation. From your ego, many branching ideas or thoughts developed. One must get to the root of it all, the fear, and realize the illusion that it is. Either the ego is real or your inner being is; only one can be real. To give life to one is to take life away from the other. But even a lack of awareness of the inner being does not for one moment change its reality. The ego was self-created. And because it was created by you, the power is also within you to undo it. This does require some assistance from Source Energy. All that is required to get into that correcting communication is willingness and desire.

Q: Is love the foundation for everything?
A: Unconditional love is the ultimate reality. It is beyond what most humans experience in their relationships. The love that comes closest to this love beyond all understanding is a mother's

love. It is completely unconditional, gives and shares freely, has no limits, and is without anger or jealousy. Unconditional love is the most powerful force in the universe and is at the core of everyone and everything. Unconditional love is the stuff the universe is made of. Even fear, when approached from an elevated point of view, is based in unconditional love because it serves a purpose, which is to awaken and enlighten.

Q: Is becoming whole and complete just a matter of realization?
A: It is a realization based in clarity and understanding. You were created whole, complete, and perfect. Nothing has to be added to you. It's a matter of awareness. It's a matter of accepting who and what you are relative to Source. You are whole. You are complete. Nothing is broken within you. You are not damaged. You need to look past the ego and find the stillness within you, your eternal, changeless, perfect, and whole self.

Q: What and where is this quantum field of consciousness?
A: The quantum field is everywhere and nowhere, or "now-here." It is the unrestricted, unlimited mind of Source Energy. It has no beginning or end. It is absolutely free of any thought whatsoever because it is simply this: limitless potential. It is the unmanifested spiritual realm. It is the birthplace of miracles, point zero for all creation. It is beyond space and time, and it is all-encompassing.

Q: Are there any intentions or affirmations that can be used for protection to ward off night terrors or paranormal phenomena when one sleeps?
A: Always remember to come from a space of confidence and gratitude when you are affirming. Come from a place of complete trust. Here are some examples:

- "Thank you for protecting me tonight and every night."
- "I am surrounded by Source's love always."
- "I am unharmable."
- "The love of the almighty fills this home and this room, now and always."

Q: The third eye seems to offer more than heightened psychic abilities. Could you expand on this?
A: An open and activated third eye is the doorway to enlightenment, which is the conscious return to the highest self. Once direct contact is made with the highest self, self-created limits are laid aside. In clearing your vibrational frequency, the mask of the ego is laid aside and the soul is allowed to express. This is a return to your spontaneous authentic self, where anything becomes possible and miracles are not only the norm, but witnessed on a moment-by-moment basis.

The sixth chakra offers clarity, and clarity is all-encompassing. It offers understanding, and understanding is all-encompassing. It reveals to you the power of forgiveness, and forgiveness is all-encompassing. It awakens dormant, spiritual forces within you that empower, enlighten, and offer insight beyond normal perception.

Q: With regards to mediumship, what are three key points to help fine-tune this ability?
A: Clarity, focus, and the willingness to surrender to the moment. Clarity allows messages to be understood more easily. Focus gives you the ability to suspend distractions, allowing you to be more present and more aware. And the act of surrender allows the ego to be put aside, thereby lessening any confusion or mixed messages.

Q: Does one shift from belief to knowing when operating through the third eye?
A: In a nutshell, yes. Knowing is a result of being one with the highest self. Beliefs are, for the most part, ego-based and apt to change. Knowing just *is*. Knowing is a reflection of the truth within you. It's the realization that Source is The All That Is. Unconditional love is The All That Is. No one can give you the truth—it just is. It's encoded within everything and everyone, as is knowing.

Q: Would it be accurate to say that we're in a dream world?
A: Relative to the spiritual realm, yes, this is a dream world. Spiritual awakening through sixth chakra activation wakes you up from the dream and the dream of excess thinking. More so, this world is a reflection of an even greater reality. The world most humans currently experience and know is a dream world because it is based in their idea of separation. An entirely new world, heaven on earth, awaits those who choose to make the shift in awareness. In one sense, you will find yourself at home with Source once you awaken.

Q: Are life and Source Energy one and the same?
A: That would be an accurate statement. Life is the divine expressing itself. Everything, the entire universe, is Source Energy expressed. You don't get a life, you *are* life. You are a part of it all, one with everything. The universe is expressing itself through you as you. You are the universe. You are life expressing as a human being while also being one with it all, and that's the miracle. You are Source Energy manifested. You are a child of the infinite, and no amount of fear or human conditioning can ever change that fact.

Q: Can our adversities and trials become our greatest opportunities?

A: There is potential in everything. There is a divine purpose in every challenge one faces. In fact, it is you who have called forth these challenges for your own evolution. You are the cause—through divine power, you are able to create and call forth your reality. If your current reality no longer aligns with who you've become, choose again. Invoke the power of intention and decision. Remember to focus on the inner being, your highest self, rather than circumstances. Create a vision for yourself; the mind is everything, and every single thing is mind. See yourself spiritually awakened and see yourself experiencing higher dimensions of consciousness. Use every adversity to grow spiritually rather than allowing them to be something that keeps you stuck and stagnant. Allow the universal force within you to express itself; free yourself.

Q: Is every human being a channel for divine expression?

A: Every human being is a divine expression of Source, but not everyone becomes a conscious channel for Source Energy. Your psychic abilities, for example, do have a mind of their own. In one sense, they are your own creations, and to be like Source Energy is to allow those abilities to express (and express spontaneously, at that). Allowing your soul to express is Source Energy being who Source Energy is. Every part of you is creative by nature, including your psychic abilities. These spiritual gifts are waiting to be freed and allowed to come to life by expressing through you.

Q: Do people who have not shed their ego have the same kind of passing as those who have?
A: Those who have not shed their ego may intensely experience the fear of death at that moment or have a difficult passing, but all of that is quickly released as the ego is shed and the soul realizes itself once more. In other words, a peaceful or turbulent passing is based in your self-awareness in that moment.

Q: If we are so much more than meets the eye, why have so few of us humans been able to activate the sixth chakra and evolve further?
A: That's an excellent question. The first thing I would say is that the ego and appearances such as the physical body are very convincing. So convincing that most people leave this world with the same consciousness they developed throughout their formative years. I would also add that humans have been conditioned over thousands of years to search without, not within. They have sought to find themselves in relationships, they have looked for deliverance outside of themselves, when in fact it's always been within them, waiting to be rediscovered. The deliverance I mention relates to the deliverance from fear, from an unfulfilled life, from sickness, doubt, and uncertainty. Enlightenment is the deliverance from all that you are not—the ego—so that you can know who and what you really are.

But don't fret, the world is in the process of awakening. Humanity is reaching a tipping point. There are human beings who are already awakened on this planet, who are demonstrating what is possible through an open third eye. They are teachers and messengers of hope, light, and love. For these masters, their work is finished; they have come to help raise the individual and collective vibrational frequency. They have put themselves through unimaginable pain and discomfort to once again shed the false self and allow the full expression of Source Energy through them. The planet's awakening is happening now in the quantum field of consciousness; remember that your potential is now, spiritual awakening is now, and sixth chakra activation is possible now.

GLOSSARY

Alignment: On a spiritual level, being in sync or lined up with your highest self in mind, body, and spirit; being in accord with your life's purpose

Authentic self: Who you are at the deepest level; also known as the soul or inner being

Automatic writing: A psychic ability that allows one to write automatically by tuning in to higher consciousness or spirit guides

Awareness: In a spiritual sense, the act of being aware of spiritual faculties or higher levels of consciousness

Belief: A thought or idea that one accepts as fact or truth; can be positive or negative

Cause: A person's thought, attitude, emotional state, and vibrational frequency that calls forth the resulted condition or effect

Chakra system: The seven main chakras that are found within the subtle body

Chakra: An energy wheel found within the subtle body; each chakra pertains to a certain organ or area of the body

Clairaudience: The ability to receive information via psychic auditory means

Claircognizance: The ability to gain knowledge through an inner knowing

Clairgustance: The ability to taste food or another substance without having to put it in your mouth

Clairsalience: The ability to smell an odor/fragrance of a person/place that is not in your immediate surroundings

Clairsentience: Similar to spiritual sonar, this ability allows for information to be received through feelings or emotion; allows for the clear reading of energy

Clairvoyance: The ability to perceive or understand people, objects, or future events through extrasensory perception

Clarity: That which is experienced by a quieted mind; a reflection of your inner being that makes way for wisdom and understanding; the state of being clear

Conditioned mind: The thinking mind based in past and future; see *ego*

Conscious thinking: The act of choosing empowering, positive thoughts through expanded awareness

Consciousness: The awareness or mind of Source that one operates from; also referred as Source Energy

Effect: The circumstances one experiences as a result from past thinking and vibrational frequency

Ego: The mind's automatic negative thinker and the source of the feeling of separation

Ego death: The end of the ego's control over your consciousness; a shift in consciousness from separation to oneness

Egoic mind: See *ego*

Emotion: A thought that has been energized through reaction; energy in motion

Energy circuits: Unseen energy pathways that allow for information to instantly travel virtually

Energy field: The energy that one operates through; can be low or high vibrating

Energy information: Information that comes in the form of a feeling or knowing

Enlightenment: A transcendent state of being; a direct experience with Source Energy where one operates through the reality of oneness

Extrasensory perception: Also known as ESP; the ability to gain information beyond the physical senses

False self: See *ego*

Fifth-dimensional reality: Oneness consciousness; the realization of the spiritual realm or quantum field; the state of enlightenment

Fourth-dimensional reality: The corridor leading to the fifth-dimensional reality; an expanded awareness that there is more to life than the manifested world

Highest self: The unmanifested self that is the source of the soul; also referred to as Source or Source Energy

Infinite intelligence: The intelligence and force that is at the source for all creation; also referred to as Source, Source Energy, universal intelligence, and universal mind

Inner being: The soul; the unmanifested essence within; see *authentic self*

Inner peace: A deep sense of calm; the result of aligning with inner stillness

Inner stillness: The reflection of your inner being; a quieted mind

Inner guidance system: An emotional inner compass and intuition all in one; a reflection of your inner being that informs you energetically when you are in or out of alignment

Intention: The expression of your will expressed in thought and/or the spoken word

Intuition: The ability to know, sense, and understand something using means beyond the five senses; based in the sixth sense or third eye chakra

Life: Source or Source Energy; life is Source Energy expressing itself

Limiting belief: Any thought or idea that lowers your energy field or vibrational frequency; a thought that limits one's potential and possibility

Local mind: A person's awareness of the local environment immediately surrounding them

Meditation: The act of focusing one's awareness

Negative thought: An automatic idea or impulse based in fear, anger, or another lower-vibrating energy

Nonlocal mind: The unbounded mind, also referred to as the universal mind; unlimited in nature

Oneness: The reality that is experienced when one goes beyond their individual ego; the feeling and knowing that you are one with everyone and everything

Outlook: One's personal view on life, whether it be positive or negative

Paradigm: A set of beliefs or ideas one has about themselves

Paranormal event: An experience that defies what is currently thought of as possible in this reality

Possibility: Something that may occur, dependent upon one's thoughts, emotions, and vibrational frequency

Potential: An ability or spiritual faculty that can be realized through greater awareness

Precognition: Advanced knowledge of an event

Psychic ability: An ability that is spiritually based using means beyond the five senses

Quantum field: The unmanifested world around you; the spiritual realm; the birthplace for miracles, potential, and possibility; see *fifth-dimensional reality*

Retrocognition: Having insight and/or knowledge of past events using extrasensory perception

Separation: Spiritually speaking, the belief or idea that one is separate from everyone and everything, including Source Energy

Shadow person: The egoic self that is left behind after a person's passing; a darker entity that is attached to this world

Single vision: The ability to see oneness in everything through an activated third eye chakra

Sixth chakra: The sixth sense; the doorway to enlightenment; also referred to as the third eye chakra or brow chakra

Sixth chakra consciousness: The consciousness or awareness experienced when this chakra is activated; an expanded awareness that can perceive higher frequencies and dimensions

Soul: See *inner being*

Source: The All That Is; a higher power; also referred to as Source Energy; see *infinite intelligence*

Spirit guide: A higher-dimensional, benevolent being that guides and supports

Spirit: The unmanifested essence of a human being; also referred to as the soul

Spiritual faculty: A spiritual or mental mechanism that can be accessed through greater awareness such as inner strength or understanding

Spiritual realm: The unmanifested world beyond this one; see *quantum field* and *fifth-dimensional reality*

Spiritual sonar: The ability to instantly receive information about your environment's energy by emitting energetic waves into the quantum field; see *clairsentience*

Stillness: See *inner stillness*

Subconscious mind: Below conscious awareness, the storage system for all that one is not conscious of

Subtle body: The energy field found in and around one's physical body that is responsible for directing universal energy into the physical body and through the chakra system

Superconscious: A transcendent state beyond human awareness; see *enlightenment*

Synchronicity: A miracle appearing as a coincidence with the intention to remind you that you are supported and guided

The All That Is: See *Source*

Third eye: See *sixth chakra*

Third-dimensional reality: An awareness strictly focused on the world that is presented through the five senses

Thought: An idea or impulse that is a precursor to emotion; can be positive or negative

Understanding: Having insight into the unseen mechanics of life such as cause and effect

Universal consciousness: The underlying awareness that encompasses all of life; also known as cosmic consciousness

Universal mind: The mind of Source Energy, unbound and unlimited

Vibrational frequency: Refers to one's energy field; based on one's quality of thought, emotion, and outlook

Wakeful meditation: The practice of being conscious and self-aware throughout the day

RECOMMENDED READING

Friedlander, John, and Gloria Hemsher. *Basic Psychic Development: A User's Guide to Auras, Chakras & Clairvoyance.* San Francisco: Red Wheel/Weiser, 2012.

Katz, Debra Lynne. *Extraordinary Psychic: Proven Techniques to Master Your Natural Psychic Abilities.* Santa Barbara, CA: Living Dreams Press, 2014.